Network Threat Assessment: Botnets
Reference Guide

Contents

Chapter 1

Botnet

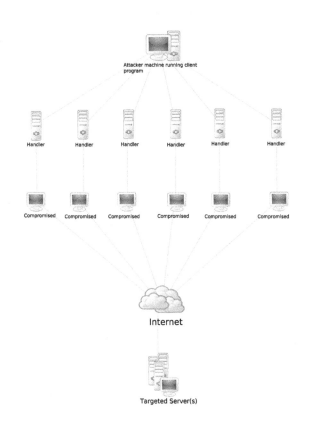

Stacheldraht botnet diagram showing a DDoS attack. (Note this is also an example of a type of client-server model of a botnet.)

A **botnet** is a number of Internet-connected computers communicating with other similar machines in which components located on networked computers communicate and coordinate their actions by command and control (C&C) or by passing messages to one another (C&C might be built into the botnet as P2P).[1] Botnets have been used many times to send spam email or participate in distributed denial-of-service attacks. The word botnet is a combination of the words robot and network. The term is usually used with a negative or malicious connotation.

1.1 Applications

1.1.1 Legal

Most of the time when botnets are in the legal area are commonly used for Distributed computing which is a field of computer science that studies distributed systems. A distributed system is a software system in which components located on networked computers communicate and coordinate their actions by passing messages. The components interact with each other in order to achieve a common goal. Three significant characteristics of distributed systems are: concurrency of components, lack of a global clock, and independent failure of components. A command and control may be present in the distributed computing but no zombie computer is present in this type of system.[2]

1.1.2 Illegal

Botnets sometimes compromise computers whose security defenses have been breached and control ceded to a third party. Each such compromised device, known as a "bot", is created when a computer is penetrated by software from a *malware* (malicious software) distribution. The controller of a botnet is able to direct the activities of these compromised computers through communication channels formed by standards-based network protocols such as IRC and Hypertext Transfer Protocol (HTTP).[3]

Botnets are increasingly rented out by cyber criminals as commodities for a variety of purposes.[4]

1.2 Architecture

The methods on which botnets are built for communications. Botnet architecture evolved over time, and not all botnets exhibit the same topology for command and control. Advanced topology is more resilient to shutdown, enumeration or discovery. However, some topologies limit the marketability of the botnet to third parties. Typical botnet topologies are star, multi-server, hierarchical and random.

1.2.1 Client–server model

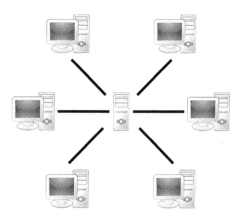

A network based on the client-server model, where individual clients request services and resources from centralized servers

The Client–server model appeared on the first types of botnets that appeared online and has usually been built on Internet Relay Chat or by using Domains or Websites which will have the commands listed for the botnet to be controlled. In IRC commands tend to be simpler and botnets tend to be smaller if built on an IRC network. Since IRC networks require low bandwidth and use simple methods for communication, they have been used to host botnets that tend to be simple in construction and have been used many times for coordinating DDoS attacks or spam campaigns while switching channels to avoid being taken down. Blocking certain keywords has sometimes proved effective in stopping a botnet based on IRC.

Most of the largest botnets that have been built tended to use domains rather than IRC in their construction.(see Rustock botnet see also Srizbi botnet.) Almost always they have been hosted with bullet proof hosting services.(See Bulletproof hosting.) Since most of the time botnets based on the Client-server model have been taken down in a matter of time, hackers have moved toward P2P as an alternative to avoid botnet takedowns.

Botnet servers are typically redundant, linked for greater redundancy so as to reduce the threat of a takedown. Actual botnet communities usually consist of one or several con-

trollers that rarely have highly developed command hierarchies; they rely on individual peer-to-peer relationships.[5]

The botnet server structure mentioned above has inherent vulnerabilities and problems. For example, finding one server with one botnet channel can often reveal the other servers, as well as their bots. A botnet server structure that lacks redundancy is vulnerable to at least the temporary disconnection of that server. However, recent IRC server software includes features to mask other connected servers and bots, eliminating that approach.

1.2.2 Peer-to-peer

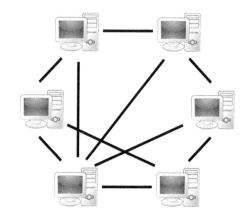

A peer-to-peer (P2P) network in which interconnected nodes ("peers") share resources amongst each other without the use of a centralized administrative system

Since most of the time IRC networks and Domains can be taken down with time, hackers have moved on to P2P as a way to make it harder to be taken down. Some have even been known to use encryption as a way to secure or lock down the botnet from others, most of the time when they use encryption it is Public-Key encryption and has presented challenges in both implementing it and breaking it.(See Gameover ZeuS See also ZeroAccess botnet.)

Some newer botnets are almost entirely P2P. Command and control is embedded into the botnet rather than relying on external servers, thus avoiding any single point of failure and evading many countermeasures.[6] Commanders can be identified just through secure keys, and all data except the binary itself can be encrypted. For example, a spyware program may encrypt all suspected passwords with a public key that is hard-coded into it, or distributed with the bot software. Only with the private key (known only by the botnet operators) can the data captured by the bot be read.

In the P2P method of command and control the bot only tends to know a list of peers of which it can send commands to and that are passed on to other peers further down the botnet. The list tends to be around 256 peers which allows it to be small enough for it to allow commands to be quickly passed on to other peers and makes it harder to disrupt the operation of the botnet while allowing it to remain online if major numbers of peers are taken down in a takedown effort.

1.3 Core components of a botnet

There are several core components in a botnet which have been used. The main ones are listed below

1.3.1 Command and control

In the field of computer security, command and control (C&C) infrastructure consists of servers and other technical infrastructure used to control malware in general, and, in particular, botnets. Command and control servers may be either directly controlled by the malware operators, or themselves run on hardware compromised by malware. Fast-flux DNS can be used as a way to make it difficult to track down the control servers, which may change from day to day. Control servers may also hop from DNS domain to DNS domain, with domain generation algorithms being used to create new DNS names for controller servers.

In some cases, computer security experts have succeeded in destroying or subverting malware command and control networks, by, among other means, seizing servers or getting them cut off from the Internet, denying access to domains that were due to be used by malware to contact its C&C infrastructure, and, in some cases, breaking into the C&C network itself. In response to this, C&C operators have resorted to using techniques such as overlaying their C&C networks on other existing benign infrastructure such as IRC or Tor, using peer-to-peer networking systems that are not dependent on any fixed servers, and using public key encryption to defeat attempts to break into or spoof the network.

1.3.2 Zombie computer

In computer science, a zombie computer is a computer connected to the Internet that has been compromised by a hacker, computer virus or trojan horse and can be used to perform malicious tasks of one sort or another under remote direction. Botnets of zombie computers are often used to spread e-mail spam and launch denial-of-service attacks. Most owners of zombie computers are unaware that their system is being used in this way. Because the owner tends to be unaware, these computers are metaphorically compared to zombies. A coordinated DDoS attack by multiple botnet machines also resembles a zombie horde attack.

1.4 Construction

This example illustrates how a botnet is created and used for malicious gain

1. A hacker purchases or builds a Trojan and/or exploit kit and uses it to start infecting users' computers, whose payload is a malicious application—the *bot*.

2. The *bot* on the infected PC logs into a particular command-and-control (C&C) server. (This allows the bot master to keep logs of how many bots are active and online.)

3. The bot master may then use the bots to gather keystrokes or use form grabbing to steal online credentials and may rent out the botnet as DDoS and/or spam as a service or sell the credentials online for a profit.

4. Depending on the quality and capability of the bots the value is increased or decreased.

1.4.1 Common features

- Most botnets currently feature distributed denial-of-service attacks in which multiple systems submit as many requests as possible to a single Internet computer or service, overloading it and preventing it from servicing legitimate requests. An example is an attack on a victim's server. The victim's server is bombarded with requests by the bots, attempting to connect to the server therefore overloading it.

- Spyware is software which sends information to its creators about a user's activities – typically passwords, credit card numbers and other information that can be sold on the black market. Compromised machines that are located within a corporate network can be worth more to the bot herder, as they can often gain access to confidential corporate information. Several targeted attacks on large corporations aimed to steal sensitive information, such as the Aurora botnet.[7]

- E-mail spam are e-mail messages disguised as messages from people, but are either advertising, annoying, or malicious.

- Click fraud occurs when the user's computer visits websites without the user's awareness to create false web traffic for personal or commercial gain.

- Bitcoin Mining has been added to some of the more recent botnets have which include bitcoin mining[8] as a feature in order to generate profits for the operator of the botnet.

The botnet controller community features a constant and continuous struggle over who has the most bots, the highest overall bandwidth, and the most "high-quality" infected machines, like university, corporate, and even government machines.[9]

1.4.2 Organization

While botnets are often named after the malware that created them, multiple botnets typically use the same malware, but are operated by different entities.[10]

A botnet's originator (known as a "bot herder" or "bot master") can control the group remotely, usually through IRC or Domains, and often for criminal purposes. This is known as the **command-and-control (C&C)**. Though rare, more experienced botnet operators program command protocols from scratch. These protocols include a server program, a client program for operation, and the program that embeds the client on the victim's machine. These communicate over a network, using a unique encryption scheme for stealth and protection against detection or intrusion into the botnet.

A bot typically runs hidden and uses a covert channel (e.g. the RFC 1459 (IRC) standard, Twitter, or IM) to communicate with its C&C server. Generally, the perpetrator has compromised multiple systems using various tools (exploits, buffer overflows, as well as others; see also RPC). Newer bots can automatically scan their environment and propagate themselves using vulnerabilities and weak passwords. Generally, the more vulnerabilities a bot can scan and propagate through, the more valuable it becomes to a botnet controller community. The process of stealing computing resources as a result of a system being joined to a "botnet" is sometimes referred to as "scrumping."

To thwart detection, some botnets are scaling back in size. As of 2006, the average size of a network was estimated at 20,000 computers.[11]

1.4.3 Recruitment

Computers can be co-opted into a botnet when they execute malicious software. This can be accomplished by luring users into making a drive-by download, exploiting web browser vulnerabilities, or by tricking the user into running a Trojan horse program, which may come from an email attachment. This malware will typically install modules that allow the computer to be commanded and controlled by the botnet's operator. After the software is downloaded, it will call home (send a reconnection packet) to the host computer. When the re-connection is made, depending on how it is written, a Trojan may then delete itself, or may remain present to update and maintain the modules. Many computer users are unaware that their computer is infected with bots.[12]

The first botnet was first acknowledged and exposed by Earthlink during a lawsuit with notorious spammer Khan C. Smith[13] in 2001 for the purpose of bulk spam accounting for nearly 25% of all spam at the time.

1.5 Countermeasures

The geographic dispersal of botnets means that each recruit must be individually identified/corralled/repaired and limits the benefits of filtering. Some botnets use free DNS hosting services such as DynDns.org, No-IP.com, and Afraid.org to point a subdomain towards an IRC server that harbors the bots. While these free DNS services do not themselves host attacks, they provide reference points (often hard-coded into the botnet executable). Removing such services can cripple an entire botnet. Some botnets implement custom versions of well-known protocols. The implementation differences can be used for detection of botnets. For example, Mega-D features a slightly modified SMTP protocol implementation for testing spam capability. Bringing down the Mega-D's SMTP server disables the entire pool of bots that rely upon the same SMTP server.[14]

Computer and network security companies have released software to counter botnets. Norton AntiBot was aimed at consumers, but most target enterprises and/or ISPs. Host-based techniques use heuristics to identify bot behavior that has bypassed conventional anti-virus software. Network-based approaches tend to use the techniques described above; shutting down C&C servers, nullrouting DNS entries, or completely shutting down IRC servers. BotHunter is software, developed with support from the U.S. Army Research Office, that detects botnet activity within a network by analysing network traffic and comparing it to patterns characteristic of malicious processes.

Some botnets are capable of detecting and reacting to attempts to investigate them, reacting perhaps with a DDoS attack on the IP address of the investigator.

Researchers at Sandia National Laboratories are analyzing botnets' behavior by simultaneously running one million Linux kernels—a similar scale to a botnet—as virtual machines on a 4,480-node high-performance computer cluster to emulate a very large network, allowing them to watch how botnets work and experiment with ways to stop them.[15]

1.6 Historical list of botnets

- Researchers at the University of California, Santa Barbara took control of a botnet that was six times smaller than expected. In some countries, it is common that users change their IP address a few times in one day. Estimating the size of the botnet by the number of IP addresses is often used by researchers, possibly leading to inaccurate assessments.[39]

1.7 See also

- Anti-spam techniques (e-mail)

- Backdoor:Win32.Hupigon

- Carna botnet

- Command and control (malware)

- Computer worm

- E-mail address harvesting

- E-mail spam

- List poisoning

- Spambot

- Spamtrap

- Timeline of computer viruses and worms

- Xor DDoS

- Zombie (computer science)

- ZeroAccess botnet

1.8 References

[1] "botnet". Retrieved 9 June 2016.

[2] "Forensics and Incident Response". www.peerlyst.com. Retrieved 3 April 2016.

[3] Ramneek, Puri (2003-08-08). "Bots &; Botnet: An Overview" (PDF). SANS Institute. Retrieved 12 November 2013.

[4] Danchev, Dancho (11 October 2013). "Novice cyberciminals offer commercial access to five mini botnets". Retrieved 28 June 2015.

[5] "what is a Botnet trojan?". DSL Reports. Retrieved 7 April 2011.

[6] Wang, Ping et al. (2010). "Peer-to-peer botnets". In Stamp, Mark & Stavroulakis, Peter. *Handbook of Information and Communication Security*. Springer. ISBN 9783642041174.

[7] "Operation Aurora — The Command Structure". Damballa.com. Archived from the original on 11 June 2010. Retrieved 30 July 2010.

[8] "Bitcoin Mining". BitcoinMining.com. Archived from the original on 30 April 2016. Retrieved 30 April 2016.

[9] "Trojan horse, and Virus FAQ". DSLReports. Retrieved 7 April 2011.

[10] Many-to-Many Botnet Relationships, *Damballa*, 8 June 2009.

[11] "Hackers Strengthen Malicious Botnets by Shrinking Them" (PDF). *Computer; News Briefs*. IEEE Computer Society. April 2006. doi:10.1109/MC.2006.136. Retrieved 12 November 2013. The size of bot networks peaked in mid-2004, with many using more than 100,000 infected machines, according to Mark Sunner, chief technology officer at MessageLabs. The average botnet size is now about 20,000 computers, he said.

[12] Teresa Dixon Murray. "Banks can't prevent cyber attacks like those hitting PNC, Key, U.S. Bank this week". Cleveland.com. Retrieved 2 September 2014.

[13] Credeur, Mary. "Atlanta Business Chronicle, Staff Writer". bizjournals.com. Retrieved 22 July 2002.

[14] C.Y. Cho, D. Babic, R. Shin, and D. Song. Inference and Analysis of Formal Models of Botnet Command and Control Protocols, 2010 ACM Conference on Computer and Communications Security.

[15] "Researchers Boot Million Linux Kernels to Help Botnet Research". IT Security & Network Security News. 2009-08-12. Retrieved 23 April 2011.

[16] "Symantec.cloud | Email Security, Web Security, Endpoint Protection, Archiving, Continuity, Instant Messaging Security" (PDF). Messagelabs.com. Retrieved 2014-01-30.

[17] Chuck Miller (2009-05-05). "Researchers hijack control of Torpig botnet". SC Magazine US. Retrieved 10 November 2011.

[18] "Storm Worm network shrinks to about one-tenth of its former size". Tech.Blorge.Com. 2007-10-21. Retrieved 30 July 2010.

[19] Chuck Miller (2008-07-25). "The Rustock botnet spams again". SC Magazine US. Retrieved 30 July 2010.

[20] Stewart, Joe. "Spam Botnets to Watch in 2009". *Secureworks.com*. SecureWorks. Retrieved 9 March 2016.

[21] "Pushdo Botnet — New DDOS attacks on major web sites — Harry Waldron — IT Security". Msmvps.com. 2010-02-02. Retrieved 30 July 2010.

[22] "New Zealand teenager accused of controlling botnet of 1.3 million computers". The H security. 2007-11-30. Retrieved 12 November 2011.

[23] "Technology | Spam on rise after brief reprieve". BBC News. 2008-11-26. Retrieved 24 April 2010.

[24] "Sality: Story of a Peer-to-Peer Viral Network" (PDF). Symantec. 2011-08-03. Retrieved 12 January 2012.

[25] "How FBI, police busted massive botnet". theregister.co.uk. Retrieved 3 March 2010.

[26] "Calculating the Size of the Downadup Outbreak — F-Secure Weblog : News from the Lab". F-secure.com. 2009-01-16. Retrieved 24 April 2010.

[27] "Waledac botnet 'decimated' by MS takedown". The Register. 2010-03-16. Retrieved 23 April 2011.

[28] Gregg Keizer (2008-04-09). "Top botnets control 1M hijacked computers". Computerworld. Retrieved 23 April 2011.

[29] "Botnet sics zombie soldiers on gimpy websites". The Register. 2008-05-14. Retrieved 23 April 2011.

[30] "Infosecurity (UK) - BredoLab downed botnet linked with Spamit.com". .canada.com. Retrieved 10 November 2011.

[31] "Research: Small DIY botnets prevalent in enterprise networks". ZDNet. Retrieved 30 July 2010.

[32] Warner, Gary (2010-12-02). "Oleg Nikolaenko, Mega-D Botmaster to Stand Trial". CyberCrime & Doing Time. Retrieved 6 December 2010.

[33] "New Massive Botnet Twice the Size of Storm — Security/Perimeter". DarkReading. Retrieved 30 July 2010.

[34] Kirk, Jeremy (Aug 16, 2012). "Spamhaus Declares Grum Botnet Dead, but Festi Surges". *PC World*.

[35] "Cómo detectar y borrar el rootkit TDL4 (TDSS/Alureon)". kasperskytienda.es. 2011-07-03. Retrieved 11 July 2011.

[36] "America's 10 most wanted botnets". Networkworld.com. 2009-07-22. Retrieved 10 November 2011.

[37] http://phys.org/news/2015-02-eu-police-malicious-network.html

[38] "Discovered: Botnet Costing Display Advertisers over Six Million Dollars per Month". Spider.io. 2013-03-19. Retrieved 21 March 2013.

[39] Espiner, Tom (2011-03-08). "Botnet size may be exaggerated, says Enisa | Security Threats | ZDNet UK". Zdnet.com. Retrieved 10 November 2011.

1.9 External links

- Wired.com How-to: Build your own botnet with open source software

- The Honeynet Project & Research Alliance, "Know your Enemy: Tracking Botnets".

- The Shadowserver Foundation - An all volunteer security watchdog group that gathers, tracks, and reports on malware, botnet activity, and electronic fraud.

- NANOG Abstract: Botnets - John Kristoff's NANOG32 Botnets presentation.

- Mobile botnets - An economic and technological assessment of mobile botnets.

- Lowkeysoft - Intrusive analysis of a web-based proxy botnet (including administration screenshots).

- EWeek.com - Is the Botnet Battle Already Lost?.

- Attack of the Bots at *Wired*

- Dark Reading - Botnets Battle Over Turf.

- ATLAS Global Botnets Summary Report - Real-time database of malicious botnet command and control servers.

- FBI LAX Press Release DOJ - FBI April 16, 2008

- Milcord Botnet Defense - DHS-sponsored R&D project that uses machine learning to adaptively detect botnet behavior at the network-level

- A Botnet by Any Other Name - SecurityFocus column by Gunter Ollmann on botnet naming.

- Botnet Bust - SpyEye Malware Mastermind Pleads Guilty, FBI

- LOIC IRC-0 - An Open-Source IRC Botnet for Network Stress Testing

- LOIC SLOW IRC - An Open-Source Botnet With Webpages and IRC as C&C

Chapter 2

0x80

This is one of the images of 0x80 included in the article. Common image programs, such as ExifTool, can easily extract the location (Roland, Oklahoma) where it was taken from IPTC metadata.

0x80 is a hacker interviewed by Brian Krebs of *The Washington Post* about his lucrative business in running "botnets", or networks of remotely controlled personal computers without the owner's consent. The article in the 2006 February *Washington Post* detailed 0x80's earnings of around $6,800 a month infecting controlled personal computers with adware and spyware in exchange for a per-computer commission.[1]

2.1 Leaked data

0x80 agreed to be interviewed for the *Post* article under the condition that he'd not be identified by name or home town.[1]

After a link to the article on Slashdot, a reader used the IPTC information encoded into the image to learn that Roland, Oklahoma had been entered as the picture's location.[2][3][4] The *Washington Post* removed all of the images from their site and commented "As you know we take our obligations with sources very seriously and I don't want to comment about any speculation about sources" in response to an interview question asking "Are you aware

that the Post failed to scrub the metadata from the images used in this article, leaving information about your town?" (question text edited by *The Washington Post*; original is not available).[5]

2.2 References

[1] Brian Krebs. "Invasion of the Computer Snatchers." The Washington Post. Washingtonpost Newsweek Interactive. 2006. Retrieved September 01, 2012 from HighBeam Research

[2] Nick Farrell, "Washington Post fails to protect Deep Throat", The Inquirer, Retrieved Feb 21 2006,

[3] Ryan Naraine, "Washington Post Caught in Metadata Gaffe?" Retrieved eWeek, Feb 22nd 2006,

[4] Steven Musil, "Hacking the hacker's identity" CNet, February 22, 2006,

[5] From interview of Brian Krebs at Washington Post

2.3 External links

- Washington Post article

- Slashdot comments exposing image metadata

- Post blog about victims of 0x80 hacking

- Possible location via Google Maps

- Cheyenne Gentlemen's Club - possible strip club mentioned in the article

- LP Bottle Express - possible gas station mentioned in the article

- Blue Ribbon Chevrolet - possible used car dealership mentioned in the article

Chapter 3

Akbot

Akbot was a computer virus that infected an estimated 1.3 million computers and added them to a botnet.[1] It was created by an 18-year-old named Owen Walker, who was charged but unconvicted in 2008.

3.1 Infection

Akbot is an IRC controlled backdoor program. It allows an outside user to take control of the infected computer. Akbot operates by joining IRC servers and the waiting for further instructions. Once installed, Akbot can be used to gather data, kill processes, or perform DDOS attacks.[2]

3.2 Sources

The author, 18-year-old New Zealand based bot master, Owen Walker ("AKILL"), was caught during an international investigation, Operation: Bot Roast, during which his home was raided by New Zealand police and an FBI agent. He was charged in April 2008, but not convicted because the court did not believe his motives to be criminal.[3]

3.3 References

[1] "New Zealand teenager accused of controlling botnet of 1.3 million computers". *Heise online*. November 30, 2007. Archived from the original on 2007-12-01.

[2] "W32/Akbot". McAfee. March 20, 2006.

[3] Shenagh Gleeson and Newstalk ZB (15 July 2008). "Conviction would harm hacker's future - judge". *The New Zealand Herald*. Retrieved 16 September 2011.

Chapter 4

Alureon

Alureon (also known as **TDSS** or **TDL-4**) is a trojan and bootkit created to steal data by intercepting a system's network traffic and searching for: banking usernames and passwords, credit card data, PayPal information, social security numbers, and other sensitive user data.[1] Following a series of customer complaints, Microsoft determined that Alureon caused a wave of BSoDs on some 32-bit Microsoft Windows systems. The update, MS10-015,[2] triggered these crashes by breaking assumptions made by the malware author(s).[3][4]

According to the research conducted by Microsoft, Alureon was the second most active botnet in the second quarter of 2010.[5]

4.1 Description

The Allure boot was first identified around 2007.[6] Personal computers are usually infected when users manually download and install Trojan software. Alureon is known to have been bundled with the rogue security software, Security Essentials 2010.[2] When the dropper is executed, it first hijacks the print spooler service (spoolsv.exe) to update the master boot record and execute a modified bootstrap routine. Then it infects low-level system drivers such as those responsible for PATA operations (atapi.sys) to implement its rootkit.

Once installed, Alureon manipulates the Windows Registry to block access to Windows Task Manager, Windows Update, and the desktop. It also attempts to disable anti-virus software. Alureon has also been known to redirect search engines to commit click fraud. Google has taken steps to mitigate this for their users by scanning for malicious activity and warning users in the case of a positive detection.[7]

The malware drew considerable public attention when a software bug in its code caused some 32-bit Windows systems to crash upon installation of security update MS10-015.[2] The malware was using a hard-coded memory address in the kernel that changed after the installation of the hotfix. Microsoft subsequently modified the hotfix to prevent installation if an Alureon infection is present,[8] The malware author(s) also fixed the bug in the code.

In November 2010, the press reported that the rootkit had evolved to the point where it was able to bypass the mandatory kernel-mode driver signing requirement of 64-bit editions of Windows 7. It did this by subverting the master boot record,[9] which made it particularly resistant on all systems to detection and removal by anti-virus software.

4.2 TDL-4

TDL-4 is sometimes used synonymously with Alureon and is also the name of the rootkit that runs the botnet.

It first appeared in 2008 as TDL-1 being detected by Kaspersky Lab in April 2008. Later version two appeared known as TDL-2 in early 2009. Some time after TDL-2 became known, emerged version three which was titled TDL-3.[10] This lead eventually to TDL-4.[11]

It was often noted by journalists as "indestructible" in 2011, although it is removable with tools such as Kaspersky's TDSSKiller.[12][13] It infects the master boot record of the target machine, making it harder to detect and remove. Major advancements include encrypting communications, decentralized controls using the Kad network, as well as deleting other malware.[14][15]

4.3 Removal

While the rootkit is generally able to avoid detection, circumstantial evidence of the infection may be found through examination of network traffic with a packet analyzer or inspection of outbound connections with a tool such as netstat. Although existing security software on a computer will occasionally report the rootkit, it often goes undetected. It may be useful to perform an offline scan of the infected system after booting an alternative operating system, such as WinPE, as the malware will attempt to prevent security software from updating. The "FixMbr" command of the Windows Recovery Console and manual replacement of "atapi.sys" could possibly be required to disable the rootkit functionality before anti-virus tools are able to find and clean an infection.

Various companies have created standalone tools which attempt to remove Alureon. Two popular tools are Microsoft Windows Defender Offline and Kaspersky TDSSKiller.

4.4   Arrests

On November 9, 2011, the United States Attorney for the Southern District of New York announced charges against six Estonian nationals who were arrested by Estonian authorities and one Russian national, in conjunction with Operation Ghost Click.[16] As of February 6, 2012, two of these individuals were extradited to New York for running a sophisticated operation that used Alureon to infect millions of computers.[17]

4.5   See also

- Conficker

- Gameover ZeuS

- Rustock botnet

- Storm botnet

- Bagle (computer worm)

- Srizbi botnet

- ZeroAccess botnet

- Botnet

- Regin (malware)

- Command and control (malware)

- Zeus (malware)

- Zombie (computer science)

4.6   References

[1] "Alureon trojan caused Windows 7 BSoD". microsoft.com. February 18, 2010. Archived from the original on 10 February 2010. Retrieved 2010-02-18.

[2] "Microsoft Security Bulletin MS10-015 - Important". Microsoft. 2010-03-17. Archived from the original on 5 June 2011. Retrieved 2011-04-25.

[3] MS10-015 Restart Issues Are the Result of a Rootkit Infection (threatpost)

[4] "More information about Alureon". symantec.com.

[5] "Most Active Botnet Families in 2Q10" (PDF). Microsoft. p. 24. Retrieved 19 August 2015.

[6] *Allureon/win32*, Microsoft, March 2007

[7] "Google warns of massive malware outbreak". Financial Post. 2011-07-20. Retrieved 2011-11-25.

[8] "Update - Restart Issues After Installing MS10-015 and the Alureon Rootkit". Microsoft Security Response Center. 2010-02-17.

[9] Goodin, Dan (2010-11-16). "World's Most Advanced Rootkit Penetrates 64-bit Windows". The Register. Archived from the original on 21 November 2010. Retrieved 2010-11-22.

[10] "TDSS".

[11] "TDL4 – Top Bot".

[12] Herkanaidu, Ram (4 July 2011). "TDL-4 Indestructible or not? - Securelist". securelist. Retrieved 28 June 2012.

[13] Golovanov, Sergey; Igor Soumenkov (27 June 2011). "TDL4 – Top Bot - Securelist". Securelist. Retrieved 28 June 2012.

[14] Reisinger, Don (30 June 2011). "TDL-4: The 'indestructible' botnet? | The Digital Home - CNET News". News.cnet.com. Retrieved 15 October 2011.

[15] ""Indestructible" TDL-4 Botnet?". Techno Globes. 2 July 2011. Archived from the original on 12 October 2011. Retrieved 16 March 2016.

[16] "Operation Ghost Click". *FBI Website*. 9 November 2011. Retrieved 14 August 2015.

[17] Finkle, Jim (8 July 2015). "Virus could black out nearly 250,000 PCs". *Reuters*. Retrieved 14 August 2015.

4.7   External links

- TDSSKiller - Removal tool by Kaspersky

- Virus:Win32/Alureon.A at Microsoft Malware Protection Center

- Backdoor.Tidserv at Symantec

- Norman TDSS Remover

- TDSS Removal

Chapter 5

Asprox botnet

The **Asprox** botnet (discovered around 2008), also known by its aliases **Badsrc** and **Aseljo**, is a botnet mostly involved in phishing scams and performing SQL injections into websites in order to spread malware.[1][2][3]

5.1 Operations

Since its discovery in 2008 the Asprox botnet has been involved in multiple high-profile attacks on various websites in order to spread malware. The botnet itself consists of roughly 15,000 infected computers as of May, 2008,[4] although the size of the botnet itself is highly variable as the controllers of the botnet have been known to deliberately shrink (and later regrow) their botnet in order to prevent more aggressive countermeasures from the IT Community.[5]

The botnet propagates itself in a somewhat unusual way, as it actively searches and infects vulnerable websites running Active Server Pages. Once it finds a potential target the botnet performs a SQL Injections on the website, inserting an IFrame which redirects the user visiting the site to a site hosting Malware.[4][6]

The botnet usually attacks in waves - the goal of each wave is to infect as many websites as possible, thus achieving the highest possible spread rate. Once a wave is completed the botnet lay dormant for an extended amount of time, likely to prevent aggressive counterreactions from the security community. The initial wave took place in July, 2008, which infected an estimated 1,000 - 2,000 pages.[2][7] An additional wave took place in October 2009, infecting an unknown amount of websites. Another wave took place in June 2010, increasing the estimated total amount of infected domains from 2,000 to an estimated 10,000 - 13,000 within a day.[8][9][10]

5.2 Notable high-profile infections

While the infection targets of the Asprox botnet are randomly determined through Google searches, some high profile websites have been infected in the past. Some of these infections have received individual coverage.

- Sony PlayStation U.S.[11]
- Adobe's Serious Magic website [11]
- Several government, healthcare and business related websites [7]

5.3 See also

- Botnet
- Malware
- E-mail spam
- Internet crime
- Internet security

5.4 References

[1] "Indian Computer Emergency Response Team". Cert-In. Archived from the original on 5 September 2010. Retrieved 2010-07-30.

[2] Sue Marquette Poremba (2008-05-15). "Asprox botnet malware morphs". SC Magazine US. Archived from the original on 1 July 2010. Retrieved 2010-07-30.

[3] Leyden, John (2009-02-03). "ASProx botnet dials into Conficker domains". *.theregister.co.uk*. London, UK: The Register. Retrieved 2014-01-09.

[4] Goodin, Dan (2008-05-14). "Botnet sics zombie soldiers on gimpy websites; More SQL injection insanity". *.theregister.co.uk*. London, UK: The Register. Retrieved 2014-01-09.

[5] Hines, Matthew (2009-10-06). "Botnets - Asprox Botnet Attacks Come Back - eWeek Security Watch". Securitywatch.eweek.com. Retrieved 2010-07-30.

[6] Michael Zino (2008-05-01). "ASCII Encoded/Binary String Automated SQL Injection Attack". bloombit.com.

[7] "Asprox Botnet Mass Attack Hits Governmental, Healthcare, and Top Business Websites". CyberInsecure.com. 2008-07-18. Retrieved 2010-07-30.

[8] David Neal. "Asprox botnet causing serious concern - V3.co.uk - formerly vnunet.com". V3.co.uk. Archived from the original on 1 July 2010. Retrieved 2010-07-30.

[9] "Researchers: Asprox Botnet Is Resurging - botnets/Attacks". DarkReading. Archived from the original on 19 July 2010. Retrieved 2010-07-30.

[10] "Papers | SpiderLabs | About Us | Trustwave" (PDF). M86security.com. 2008-10-29. Retrieved 2014-01-09.

[11] "Sony PlayStation's site SQL injected, redirecting to rogue security software". ZDNet. 2008-07-02. Archived from the original on 12 August 2010. Retrieved 2010-07-30.

Chapter 6

Bagle (computer worm)

Bagle (also known as Beagle) is a mass-mailing computer worm affecting all versions of Microsoft Windows. The first strain, **Bagle.A**, did not propagate widely. A second variant, **Bagle.B**, is considerably more virulent.

Bagle uses its own SMTP engine to mass-mail itself as an attachment to recipients gathered from the infected computer. It copies itself to the Windows system directory (Bagle.A as bbeagle.exe, Bagle.B as au.exe) and opens a backdoor on TCP port 6777 (Bagle.A) or 8866 (Bagle.B). It does not mail itself to addresses containing certain strings such as "@hotmail.com", "@msn.com", "@microsoft" or "@avp".

The initial strain, Bagle.A, was first sighted on January 18, 2004. It was not widespread and stopped spreading after January 28, 2004.

The second strain, Bagle.B, was first sighted on February 17, 2004. It was much more widespread and appeared in large numbers; Network Associates rated it a "medium" threat. It is designed to stop spreading after February 25, 2004.

Subsequent variants have later been discovered. Although they have not all been successful, a number remain notable threats.

Some of these variants contain the following text:

"Greetz to antivirus companies In a difficult world, In a nameless time, I want to survive, So, you will be mine!! -- Bagle Author, 29.04.04, Germany."

This has led some people think the worm originated in Germany.

Since 2004, the threat risk from these variants has been changed to "low" due to decreased prevalence. However, Windows users are warned to watch out for it.

6.1 Botnet

The Bagle botnet (Initial discovery early 2004[1][2]), also known by its aliases **Beagle**, **Mitglieder** and **Lodeight**,[3] is a botnet mostly involved in proxy-to-relay e-mail spam.

The Bagle botnet consists of an estimated 150,000-230,000 [4] computers infected with the Bagle Computer worm. It was estimated that the botnet was responsible for about 10.39% of the worldwide spam volume on December 29, 2009, with a surge up to 14% on New Year's Day,[5] though the actual percentage seems to rise and drop rapidly.[6] As of April 2010 it is estimated that the botnet sends roughly 5.7 billion spam messages a day, or about 4.3% of the global spam volume.[4]

6.2 See also

- Command and control (malware)
- Zombie (computer science)
- Netsky (computer worm)
- Botnet
- Malware
- E-mail spam
- Internet crime
- Internet security
- McColo
- Operation: Bot Roast
- Srizbi Botnet
- Alureon
- Conficker

- Gameover ZeuS

- Storm botnet

- Rustock botnet

- ZeroAccess botnet

- Regin (malware)

- Zeus (malware)

6.3   References

[1] "The Bagle botnet". Securelist. Retrieved 2010-07-30.

[2] "A Little Spam With Your Bagle?". M86 Security. 2009-06-05. Retrieved 2010-07-30.

[3] "Bagle". M86 Security. 2009-06-05. Retrieved 2010-07-30.

[4] http://www.messagelabs.com/mlireport/MLI_2010_04_Apr_FINAL_EN.pdf

[5] Dan Raywood. "New botnet threats emerge in the New Year from Lethic and Bagle". SC Magazine UK. Retrieved 2010-07-30.

[6] "New Spamming Botnet On The Rise". DarkReading. Retrieved 2010-07-30.

Chapter 7

BASHLITE

BASHLITE (also known as Gafgyt, Lizkebab, BASH-LITE, Torlus and LizardStresser.) is a piece of Malware written in C which infects Linux systems in order to launch distributed denial-of-service attacks.[1]

7.1 See also

- Low Orbit Ion Cannon A stress test tool that has been used for DDoS attacks

- High Orbit Ion Cannon The replacement for LOIC used in DDoS attacks

- Fork bomb

- Denial-of-service attack

- Slowloris (computer security)

- ReDoS

7.2 References

[1] Cimpanu, Catalin (Aug 30, 2016). "There's a 120,000-Strong IoT DDoS Botnet Lurking Around". Softpedia. Retrieved 19 October 2016.

Chapter 8

Bot herder

Bot herders[1] are Hackers who use automated techniques to scan specific network ranges and find vulnerable systems, such as machines without current security patches, on which to install their bot program. The infected machine then has become one of many zombies[2] in a botnet and responds to commands given by the bot herder, usually via an Internet Relay Chat channel.

One of the new bot herders includes the controller of Conficker.

A bot herder usually uses a pseudonym to keep themselves anonymous, and may use proxy servers, shell accounts and bouncers to conceal their IP address thus maintaining anonymity.

8.1 See also

- Internet bot

- Botnet

8.2 References

[1] "Microsoft goes bot herder hunting in streets of Russia".

[2] "Bot herder pleads guilty to 'zombie' sales".

Chapter 9

Bredolab botnet

The **Bredolab botnet**, also known by its alias **Oficla**,[1] was a Russian[2] botnet mostly involved in viral e-mail spam. Before the botnet was eventually dismantled in November 2010 through the seizure of its command and control servers, it was estimated to consist of millions of zombie computers.[3][4][5]

9.1 Operations

Though the earliest reports surrounding the Bredolab botnet originate from May 2009 (when the first malware samples of the Bredolab trojan horse were found) the botnet itself did not rise to prominence until August 2009, when there was a major surge in the size of the botnet.[6][7] Bredonet's main form of propagation was through sending malicious e-mails that included malware attachments which would infect a computer when opened, effectively turning the computer into another zombie controlled by the botnet. At its peak, the botnet was capable of sending 3.6 billion viral emails every day.[8] The other main form of propagation was through the use of drive-by downloads - a method which exploits security vulnerabilities in software. This method allowed the botnet to bypass software protection in order to facilitate downloads without the user being aware of them.[9]

The main income of the botnet was generated through leasing parts of the botnet to third parties who could subsequently use these infected systems for their own purposes, and security researchers estimate that the owner of the botnet made up to $139,000 a month from botnet related activities.[4][10][11] Due to the rental business strategy, the payload of Bredolab has been very diverse, and ranged from scareware to malware and e-mail spam.[12]

9.1.1 Dismantling and aftermath

On 25 October 2010, a team of Dutch law enforcement agents seized control of 143 servers which contained three command & control servers, one database server and several management servers from the Bredolab botnet in a datacenter from LeaseWeb,[13] effectively removing the botnet herder's ability to control the botnet centrally.[2][12][14] In an attempt to regain control over his botnet, the botnet herder utilized 220,000 computers which were still under his control, to unleash a DDoS attack on LeaseWeb servers, though these attempts were ultimately in vain.[15] After taking control over the botnet, the law enforcement team utilized the botnet itself to send a message to owners of infected computers, stating that their computer was part of the botnet.[8][16]

Subsequently Armenian law enforcement officers arrested an Armenian citizen, Georgy Avanesov,[4][17] on the basis of being the suspected mastermind behind the botnet. The suspect denied any such involvement in the botnet.[11][12] He was sentenced to four years in prison in May 2012.[18]

While the seizure of the command and control servers severely disrupted the botnet's ability to operate,[19] the botnet itself is still partially intact, with command and control servers persisting in Russia and Kazakhstan.[16] Security firm FireEye believes that a secondary group of botnet herders has taken over the remaining part of the botnet for their own purposes, possibly a previous client who reverse engineered parts of the original botnet creator's code. Even so, the group noted that the botnet's size and capacity has been severely reduced by the law enforcement intervention.[10][13][20]

9.2 References

[1] Search the malware encyclopedia: Bredolab, Microsoft.com

[2] Dan Raywood (2010-10-26). "Bredolab botnet taken down after Dutch intervention". SC Magazine UK. Retrieved 2012-01-28.

[3] James Wray and Ulf Stabe (2010-10-28). "Researchers: Bredolab still lurking, though severely injured (Update 3) - Security". Thetechherald.com. Retrieved 2012-01-28.

[4] "Infosecurity (UK) - BredoLab downed botnet linked with Spamit.com". Infosecurity-magazine.com. 2010-11-01. Retrieved 2012-01-28.

[5] Help Net Security (2010-11-02). "The aftermath of the Bredolab botnet shutdown". Net-security.org. Retrieved 2012-01-28.

[6] "Security Threat Reports - Research Analysis - Trend Micro USA" (PDF). Us.trendmicro.com. Retrieved 2012-01-28.

[7] "Trojan.Bredolab". Symantec. Retrieved 2012-01-28.

[8] "Infosecurity (USA) - Dutch government shuts down Bredolab botnet". Infosecurity-us.com. 2010-10-26. Retrieved 2012-01-28.

[9] "Trojan.Bredolab Technical Details". Symantec. Retrieved 2012-01-28.

[10] Bredolab Down but Far from Out After Botnet Takedown, 28 October 2010

[11] "More Bredolab arrests may occur, say Dutch prosecutors - Techworld.com". News.techworld.com. Retrieved 2012-01-28.

[12] Schwartz, Mathew J. (2010-10-29). "Bredolab Botnet Still Spewing Malware - Bredolab Botnet". InformationWeek. Retrieved 2012-01-28.

[13] de Graaf, JD (2012). "BREDOLAB: Shopping in the Cybercrime Underworld" (PDF). *ICDF2C Conference*. Springer-Verlag.

[14] Josh Halliday (2010-10-26). "Suspected Bredolab worm mastermind arrested in Armenia | Technology". London: guardian.co.uk. Retrieved 2012-01-28.

[15] "Suspected Bredolab Botnet Runner Arrested in Armenia - Softpedia". News.softpedia.com. 2010-10-26. Retrieved 2012-01-28.

[16] Undead Bredolab zombie network lashes out from the grave, 29 October 2010

[17] "Bredolab Mastermind Was Key Spamit.com Affiliate — Krebs on Security". Krebsonsecurity.com. 2010-10-30. Retrieved 2012-01-28.

[18] "Russian spam mastermind jailed for creating botnet". *BBC News*. 24 May 2012. Retrieved 24 May 2012.

[19] "Bredolab, dead, dying or dormant? » CounterMeasures". Countermeasures.trendmicro.eu. 2010-10-26. Retrieved 2012-01-28.

[20] Atif Mushtaq on 2010.10.26 (2010-10-26). "FireEye Malware Intelligence Lab: Bredolab - Severely Injured but not dead". Blog.fireeye.com. Retrieved 2012-01-28.

Chapter 10

Carna botnet

World map of 24-hour relative average utilization of IPv4 addresses observed using ICMP ping requests by Carna botnet, June - October 2012

The **Carna botnet** was a botnet of 420,000 devices created by an anonymous hacker to measure the extent of the Internet in what the creator called the "**Internet Census of 2012**".

10.1 Data collection

The data was collected by infiltrating Internet devices, especially routers, that used a default password or no password at all.[1][2] It was named after Carna, "the Roman goddess for the protection of inner organs and health".[3]

It was compiled into a gif portrait to display Internet use around the world over the course of 24 hours. The data gathered included only the IPv4 address space and not the IPv6 address space.[4][5]

The Carna Botnet creator believes that with a growing number of IPv6 hosts on the Internet, 2012 may have been the last time a census like this was possible.[3]

10.2 Results

Of the 4.3 billion possible IPv4 addresses, Carna Botnet found a total of 1.3 billion addresses in use, including 141 million that were behind a firewall and 729 million that returned reverse domain name system records. The remaining 2.3 billion IPv4 addresses are probably not used.[3][6]

An earlier first Internet census by the USDHS LANDER-study had counted 187 million visible Internet hosts in 2006.[7][8]

10.3 Number of hosts by top level domain

Amongst other, Carna Botnet counted the number of hosts with reverse DNS names observed from May to October 2012. The top 20 Top Level Domains were:

10.4 References

[1] Stöcker, Christian; Horchert, Judith (2013-03-22). "Mapping the Internet: A Hacker's Secret Internet Census". *Spiegel Online.*

[2] Kleinman, Alexis (2013-03-22). "The Most Detailed, GIF-Based Map Of The Internet Was Made By Hacking 420,000 Computers". *Huffington Post.*

[3] Internet Census 2012: Port scanning /0 using insecure embedded devices, Carna Botnet, June - Oktober 2012

[4] Read, Max (2013-03-21). "This Illegally Made, Incredibly Mesmerizing Animated GIF Is What the Internet Looks Like". *Gawker.*

[5] Thomson, Iain (2013-03-19). "Researcher sets up illegal 420,000 node botnet for IPv4 internet map". *The Register.*

[6] Guerilla researcher created epic botnet to scan billions of IP addresses With 9TB of data, survey is one of the most

exhaustive — and illicit — ever done. by Dan Goodin, arstechnica, Mar 20, 2013

[7] Exploring Visible Internet Hosts through Census and Survey ("LANDER" study) by John Heidemann, Yuri Pradkin, Ramesh Govindan, Christos Papadopoulos, Joseph Bannister. USC/ISI Technical Report ISI-TR-2007-640. see also http://www.isi.edu/ant/address/ and video

[8] Forschung mit illegalem Botnetz: Die Vermessung des Internets Christian Stöcker, Judith Horchert, Der Spiegel, 21.03.2013

[9] Top Level Domains. Internet Census 2012

10.5   External links

- Internet Census 2012: Port scanning /0 using insecure embedded devices, Carna Botnet, June — October 2012

- All of the data can be found on GitHub, BitBucket, SourceForge, and Interent Archive.

Chapter 11

Coreflood

Coreflood is a trojan horse and botnet created by a group of Russian hackers and released in 2010. The FBI included on its list of infected systems "approximately 17 state or local government agencies, including one police department; three airports; two defense contractors; five banks or financial institutions; approximately 30 colleges or universities; approximately 20 hospital or health care companies; and hundreds of businesses."[1] It is present on more than 2.3 million computers worldwide and as of May 2011 remains a threat.

11.1 Background

Backdoor.Coreflood is a trojan horse that opens a back door on the compromised computer. It acts as a keylogger and gathers user information.[2]

11.2 Current status

The FBI has the capability, and recently authorization from the courts, to delete Coreflood from infected computers after receiving written consent. The FBI has reduced the size of the botnet by 90% in the United States and 75% around the world.[3]

11.3 References

[1] http://blogs.usdoj.gov/blog/archives/1320

[2] "Backdoor.Coreflood". Symantec. November 29, 2002. Retrieved May 3, 2011.

[3] "US authorities to delete Coreflood bot from computers.". April 29, 2011. Retrieved May 2, 2011.

Chapter 12

Cutwail botnet

The **Cutwail botnet**, founded around 2007,[1] is a botnet mostly involved in sending spam e-mails. The bot is typically installed on infected machines by a Trojan component called **Pushdo**.[2] It affects computers running Microsoft Windows.[3]

12.1 History

In June, 2009 it was estimated that the Cutwail botnet was the largest botnet in terms of the amount of infected hosts. Security provider MessageLabs estimated that the total size of the botnet was around 1.5 to 2 million individual computers, capable of sending 74 billion spam messages a day, or 51 million every minute, equal to 46.5% of the worldwide spam volume.[2][4]

In February 2010 the botnet's activities were slightly altered when it started a DDoS attack against 300 major sites, including the CIA, FBI, Twitter and Paypal. The reasons for this attack weren't fully understood, and some experts described it as an "accident", mainly due to the lack of damage and disruption, along with the infrequency of the attacks.[5]

In August 2010, researchers from University of California, Santa Barbara and Ruhr University Bochum attempted to take down the botnet, and managed to take offline 20 of the 30 Command and Control servers that the botnet was using.[2]

12.2 Structure

Cutwail is a fairly simple botnet. The bots connect directly to the command and control server, and receive instructions about the emails they should send. After they are done with their task, the bots report back to the spammer exact statistics on the number of emails that were delivered, and on which and how many errors were reported.[2]

12.3 Operations

The Cutwail botnet is known as "0bulk Psyche Evolution" in the underground market. Spammers can rent an instance of the botnet for a fee, and use it to send their own spam campaigns. The services offered by the botnet were advertised on the Russian underground forum "spamdot.biz", that was taken down in 2010. As of June 2010, at least 8 different spam groups were using the botnet to deliver junk mail.[2]

12.4 See also

- Operation: Bot Roast
- McColo
- Srizbi Botnet
- Botnet

12.5 References

[1] Robert Jaques (October 1, 2007). "Angelina Jolie 'nudes' fuel malware spike". V3.co.uk.

[2] Brett Stone-Gross; Thorsten Holz; Gianluca Stringhini; Giovanni Vigna (March 29, 2011). "The Underground Economy of Spam: A Botmaster's Perspective of Coordinating Large-Scale Spam Campaigns" (PDF). USENIX.

[3] http://www.microsoft.com/security/portal/threat/encyclopedia/entry.aspx?Name=Backdoor%3AWin32%2FPushdo.A#tab=2. Missing or empty |title= (help)

[4] Harry Waldron (February 2, 2010). "Pushdo Botnet - New DDOS attacks on major web sites". *Computer Security News (blog)*.

[5] Kirk, Jeremy (2010-02-03). "Pushdo botnet pummels more than 300 Web sites". Itbusiness.ca. Retrieved 2010-04-21.

12.6 External links

- Technical study of the Pushdo trojan

Chapter 13

Domain generation algorithm

Domain generation algorithms (DGA) are algorithms seen in various families of malware that are used to periodically generate a large number of domain names that can be used as rendezvous points with their command and control servers. The large number of potential rendezvous points makes it difficult for law enforcement to effectively shut down botnets, since infected computers will attempt to contact some of these domain names every day to receive updates or commands. By using public-key cryptography, it is unfeasible for law enforcement and other actors to mimic commands from the malware controllers as some worms will automatically reject any updates not signed by the malware controllers.

For example, an infected computer could create thousands of domain names such as: *www.<gibberish>.com* and would attempt to contact a portion of these with the purpose of receiving an update or commands.

Embedding the DGA instead of a list of previously-generated (by the command and control server(s)) domains in the unobfuscated binary of the malware protects against a strings dump that could be fed into a network blacklisting appliance preemptively to attempt to restrict outbound communication from infected hosts within an enterprise.

The technique was popularized by the family of worms Conficker.a and .b which, at first generated 250 domain names per day. Starting with Conficker.C, the malware would generate 50,000 domain names every day of which it would attempt to contact 500, giving an infected machine a 1% possibility of being updated every day if the malware controllers registered only one domain per day. To prevent infected computers from updating their malware, law enforcement would have needed to pre-register 50,000 new domain names every day.

Recently, the technique has been adopted by other malware authors. According to network security firm Damballa, the top 5 most prevalent DGA-based crimeware families are Conficker, Murofet, BankPatch, Bonnana and Bobax.[1]

It can also combine words from a dictionary to generate domains using a web service through a web API.

13.1 Example

def generate_domain(year, month, day): """"Generates a domain name for the given date.""" domain = "" for i in range(16): year = ((year ^ 8 * year) >> 11) ^ ((year & 0xFFFFFFF0) << 17) month = ((month ^ 4 * month) >> 25) ^ 16 * (month & 0xFFFFFFF8) day = ((day ^ (day << 13)) >> 19) ^ ((day & 0xFFFFFFFE) << 12) domain += chr(((year ^ month ^ day) % 25) + 97) return domain

E.g., on January 7th, 2014, this method would generate the domain name intgmxdeadnxuyla, while the following day, it would return axwscwsslmiagfah. This simple example was in fact used by malware like CryptoLocker, before it switched to a more sophisticated variant.

13.2 See also

- Botnet

- Conficker

- Zeus (Trojan horse)

- Srizbi botnet

- Command and control (malware)

13.3 References

[1] "Top-5 Most Prevalent DGA-based Crimeware Families" (PDF). Damballa. p. 4.

13.4 Further reading

- Phillip Porras, Hassen Saidi, Vinod Yegneswaran (2009-03-19). "An Analysis of Conficker's Logic and Rendezvous Points". *Malware Threat Center*. SRI International Computer Science Laboratory. Retrieved 2013-06-14.

- Lucian Constantin (2012-02-27). "Malware Authors Expand Use of Domain Generation Algorithms to Evade Detection". *PC World*. Retrieved 2013-06-14.

- Detecting Algorithimically Generated Malicious Domain Names

- DGAs in the Hands of Cyber-Criminals - Examining the state of the art in malware evasion techniques

- DGAs and Cyber-Criminals: A Case Study

- How Criminals Defend Their Rogue Networks, Abuse.ch

Chapter 14

Donbot botnet

Donbot, also known by its aliases **Buzus** and **Bachsoy**,[1] is a botnet mostly involved in sending pharmaceutical and stock-based e-mail spam.[2][3]

The Donbot botnet is thought to consist of roughly 125,000 individual computers,[2] which combined send 800 million spam messages a day.[4] This amount equals about 1.3% of the estimated total global spam volume[5] of 230 billion messages a day,[6] though the botnet has known spikes where it accounted for up to 4% of the total spam volume.[7]

14.1 See also

- Malware

- Internet crime

- Internet security

- Internet spam

14.2 References

[1] "Donbot". M86 Security. April 20, 2009. Retrieved July 30, 2010.

[2] Stewart, Joe (2009-01-13). "Spam Botnets to Watch in 2009 | Dell SecureWorks". *Secureworks.com*. Dell. Retrieved 2014-01-09.

[3] Aharon Etengoff (August 28, 2009). "Nefarious Donbot spews URL-shortened spam". TG Daily. Retrieved July 30, 2010."'Donbot' launches pump-and-dump run > Botnet > Vulnerabilities & Exploits > News > SC Magazine Australia/NZ". Securecomputing.net.au. Retrieved July 30, 2010.

[4] "The top 10 spam botnets: New and improved | 10 Things | TechRepublic.com". Blogs.techrepublic.com.com. February 25, 2010. Archived from the original on August 29, 2012. Retrieved July 30, 2010.

[5] "Rustock - The King of All Other Botnets". SPAMfighter. January 1, 1990. Retrieved July 30, 2010.

[6] "The top 10 'most wanted' spam-spewing botnets". Networkworld.com. Retrieved July 30, 2010.

[7] Shaun Nichols in San Francisco. "Botnet begins social networking spam run - V3.co.uk - formerly vnunet.com". V3.co.uk. Retrieved July 30, 2010.

Chapter 15

Festi

Festi is a rootkit and a botnet created on its basis. It works under operating systems of the Windows family. Autumn of 2009[1][2] was the first time Festi came into the view of the companies engaged in the development and sale of antivirus software. At this time it was estimated that the botnet itself consisted of roughly 25.000 infected machines, while having a spam volume capacity of roughly 2.5 billion spam emails a day.[3][4][5] Festi showed the greatest activity in 2011-2012.[6][7] More recent estimates - dated August 2012 - display that the botnet is sending spam from 250,000 unique IP addresses, a quarter of the total amount of one million detected IP's sending spam mails.[8] The main functionality of botnet Festi is spam sending and implementation of cyberattacks like "distributed denial of service".[9]

15.1   Distribution Methods

Distribution is carried with scheme PPI (Pay-Per-Install)[10] use. For preventing of detection by antiviruses the loader extends ciphered[10] that complicates signature based detection.

15.2   Architecture

All represented data about the architecture of botnet we have gathered from research ESET antivirus company.[10][11][12] The loader downloads and sets up a bot which represents a kernel-mode driver which adds itself in the list of the drivers which are launching together with an operating system. On a hard disk drive only the part of a bot is stored which is responsible for communication with command center and loading of modules. After starting the bot periodically asks the command center for receiving a configuration, loading of the modules and the jobs necessary for execution.

15.2.1   Modules

From the researches which have been carried out by specialists of the antivirus company ESET, it is known that Festi has at least two modules. One of them intends for spam sending (BotSpam.dll), another for implementation of cyberattacks like "distributed denial of service" (BotDoS.dll). The module for implementation of cyberattacks like "distributed denial of service" supports the following types of cyberattacks, namely: TCP-flood, UDP-flood, DNS-flood, HTTP(s)-flood, and also flood packets with a random number in the issue of the used protocol.

The expert from the "Kaspersky Lab" researching botnet drew an output that there are more modules, but not all from them are used. Their list includes the module for socks-server implementation (BotSocks.dll) with the TCP and UDP protocols, the module for remote viewing and control of the computer of the user (BotRemote.dll), the module implementing search on a disk of the remote computer and in a local area network (BotSearch.dll) to which the remote computer is connected, grabber-modules for all browsers known at present time (BotGrabber.dll).

Modules are never saved on a hard disk drive that does almost impossible their detection.

15.2.2   Network Interaction

The bot uses client-server model and for functioning implements own protocol of network interaction with command center which is used for receiving a configuration of a botnet, loading of modules, and also for obtaining jobs from command center and notification of command center about their execution. Data are encoded that interferes the determination of contents of network traffic.

15.2.3 Protection against Detection and Debugging

In case of installation the bot switches off a system firewall, hides the kernel-mode driver and the keys of the system registry necessary for loading and operation, protects itself and registry keys from deleting. Operation with a network occurs at a low level that allows to bypass network filters of the antivirus software easily. The use of network filters is observed to prevent their installation. The bot checks, whether it is launched under the virtual machine, in case of positive result of the check, it stops the activities. Festi periodically checks existence of a debugger and is able to remove breakpoints.

15.2.4 The Object-Oriented Approach to Development

Festi is created with use of object-oriented technology of software development that strongly complicates researches by a method of the reverse engineering and does a bot easily ported for other operating systems.

15.2.5 Control

All control of botnet Festi is implemented by means of web interface and is carried out via browser.

15.3 Who Stands behind Festi

According to specialists of the antivirus company ESET,[12] to American journalist and blogger Brian Krebs,[13] the expert in information security field, according to American journalist of The New York Times newspaper Andrew Kramer,[14] and also from the sources close to Russian intelligence services, the architect and the developer of botnet Festi — Russian hacker Igor Artimovich.

15.4 Conclusion

In conclusion, it is possible to tell that botnet Festi was one of the most powerful botnets for sending spam and carrying out attacks like "distributed denial of service". The principles by which Festi botnet is constructed increase bot lifetime in the system as much as possible, hinder with bot detection by the antivirus software and network filters. The mechanism of modules allows to expand functionality of botnet in any side by means of creation and loading of necessary modules for achievement of different purposes, and the object-oriented approach to development complicates botnet researching with use of methods of the reverse engineering and gives the chance of bot porting on other operating systems through an accurate demarcation of specific to a concrete operating system functionality and remaining logic of bot. Powerful systems of counteraction to detection and debugging make Festi bot almost invisible and stealthy. The system of bindings and use of reserve command centers gives the chance of restoration of control over a botnet after change of command center. Festi is an atypical example of malicious software as the authors approached the process of its development extremely seriously.[15]

15.5 See also

- Botnets
- Malware
- Cyberwarfare

15.6 References

[1] Lewis, Daren (November 5, 2009). "Festi Botnet spins up to become one of the main spamming botnets". *Symantec Connect.*

[2] Kaplan, Dan (November 6, 2009). "Festi botnet appears". *SC Magazine.*

[3] Jackson Higgins, Kelly (November 6, 2009). "New Spamming Botnet On The Rise - Dark Reading". *darkreading.*

[4] Wattanajantra, Asavin (November 6, 2009). "'Festi' growing to become spambot heavyweight". *ITPRO.*

[5] "Botnet Festi Rising Tremendously". *SPAMfighter.* November 18, 2009.

[6] Kirk, Jeremy (August 16, 2012). "Spamhaus Declares Grum Botnet Dead, but Festi Surges". *PC World.*

[7] Kirk, Jeremy (August 17, 2012). "Spamhaus declares Grum botnet dead, but Festi surges". *PC Advisor.*

[8] Saarinen, Juha (Aug 20, 2012). "Festi botnet cranks up spam volumes". *ITNews.*

[9] "Festi botnet helps launch denial-of-service 'DDoS' attack". *Stop Hackers.* June 13, 2012.

[10] Matrosov, Aleksandr (May 11, 2012). "King of Spam: Festi botnet analysis". *ESET.*

[11] Rodionov, Eugene (2011). "Festi botnet analysis and investigation" (PDF). *ESET.*

[12] Matrosov, Aleksandr (November 12–14, 2012). "Festi Botnet Analysis & Investigation" (PDF). *AVAR 2012.*

[13] Krebs, Brian (June 12, 2012). "Who Is the 'Festi' Botmaster?". *Krebs On Security.*

[14] Kramer, Andrew (September 2, 2013). "Online Attack Leads to Peek Into Spam Den". *The New York Times.*

[15] "Festi: malicious and incorporeal". *Xakep Magazine.* September 2012.

15.7 External links

- Top 10 botnets and their impact, December 9, 2009, Top 10 botnets and their impact, Help Net Security

- The top 10 'most wanted' spam-spewing botnets Rustock, Mega-D, Festi, Pushdo among worst botnet offenders, July 15, 2010, Ellen Messmer, Network World

- The New Era of Botnets, White Paper

- Festi botnet takes over following Grum shutdown, August 17, 2012, ComputerWorld UK

- Spam botnets: The fall of Grum and the rise of Festi, August 16, 2012, Thomas Morrison, SPAMHAUS

- Spamhaus: Grum Dead, Festi Alive and Well August 22, 2012, Malcolm James, All Spammed Up

- The Global Botnet Threat, November 14, 2012, MacAfee

Chapter 16

Festi botnet

The **Festi botnet**, also known by its alias of **Spamnost**, is a botnet mostly involved in email spam and denial of service attacks.

16.1 History and operations

The Festi botnet was first discovered around Autumn 2009.[1] At this time it was estimated that the botnet itself consisted of roughly 25000 infected machines, while having a spam volume capacity of roughly 2.5 billion spam emails a day.[2] More recent estimates - dated August 2012 - display that the botnet is sending spam from 250000 unique IP addresses,[3] a quarter of the total amount of 1 million detected IP's sending spam mails.[4] Besides being capable of sending email spam, research into the Festi botnet demonstrated that it is also capable of performing denial of service attacks.[5][6]

16.2 See also

- Malware

- Internet crime

- Internet security

16.3 References

[1] Kaplan, Dan (November 6, 2009). "Festi botnet appears". *SC Magazine*. Retrieved 1 January 2013.

[2] Jackson Higgins, Kelly (Nov 6, 2009). "New Spamming Botnet On The Rise - Dark Reading". *darkreading*. Retrieved 1 January 2013.

[3] Kirk, Jeremy (Aug 16, 2012). "Spamhaus Declares Grum Botnet Dead, but Festi Surges". *PC World*. Retrieved 1 January 2013.

[4] Saarinen, Juha (Aug 20, 2012). "Festi botnet cranks up spam volumes". *ITNews*. Retrieved 1 January 2013.

[5] Krebs, Brian (June 2012). "Who Is the 'Festi' Botmaster?". *Krebs on Security*. Retrieved 1 January 2013.

[6] Matrosov, Aleksandr (May 11, 2012). "King of Spam: Festi botnet analysis". *ESET*. Retrieved 1 January 2013.

16.4 External links

- Analysis of the Festi botnet by Eset

Chapter 17

Gameover ZeuS

Not to be confused with Zeus (malware).

Gameover ZeuS is a peer-to-peer botnet based on components from the earlier ZeuS trojan. It is believed to have been spread through use of the Cutwail botnet.[1]

Unlike its predecessor the ZeuS trojan, Gameover ZeuS uses an encrypted peer-to-peer communication system to communicate between its nodes and its command and control servers, greatly reducing its vulnerability to law enforcement operations.[1] The algorithm used appears to be modeled on the Kademlia P2P protocol.[2]

According to a report by Symantec, Gameover Zeus has largely been used for banking fraud and distribution of the CryptoLocker ransomware.[3]

In early June 2014, the U.S. Department of Justice announced that an international inter-agency collaboration named Operation Tovar had succeeded in temporarily cutting communication between Gameover ZeuS and its command and control servers.[4][5]

On 24 February 2015, the FBI announced a reward of up to $3 million in exchange for information regarding Russian cyber criminal Evgeniy Bogachev over his association with Gameover ZeuS.[6] [7]

Bitdefender has identified two Gameover ZeuS variants in the wild: one of them generates 1,000 domains per day and the other generates 10,000 per day.[8]

Fox-IT helped to end the Gameover ZeuS criminal network.[9]

17.1   See also

- Conficker

- Command and control (malware)

- Operation Tovar

- Timeline of computer viruses and worms

- Tiny Banker Trojan

- Torpig

- Zeus (malware)

- Zombie (computer science)

17.2   References

[1] Brian Krebs (2 June 2014). "'Operation Tovar' Targets 'Gameover' ZeuS Botnet, CryptoLocker Scourge". Krebs on Security.

[2] By Counter Threat Unit™ (CTU) Research Team. "Gameover Zeus re-emerges without peer-to-peer capability". *Secureworks.com*. SecureWorks. Retrieved 9 March 2016.

[3] "International Takedown Wounds Gameover Zeus Cybercrime Network". Symantec. 2 June 2014.

[4] John E. Dunn (2 June 2014). "Operation Tovar disconnects Gameover Zeus and CryptoLocker malware - but only for two weeks". TechWorld.

[5] "U.S. Leads Multi-National Action Against "Gameover Zeus" Botnet and "Cryptolocker" Ransomware, Charges Botnet Administrator". U.S. Department of Justice. 2 June 2014.

[6] Perez, Evan. "U.S. puts $3 million reward for Russian cyber criminal". *CNN*. CNN. Retrieved 24 February 2015.

[7] "US offers $3m reward for arrest of Russian hacker Evgeniy Bogachev". BBC.

[8] Cosovan, Doina (6 August 2014). "Gameover Zeus Variants Targeting Ukraine, US". BitDefender LABS.

[9] "End of Gameover ZeuS". Automatiseringsgids. 8 August 2015.

Chapter 18

Grum botnet

The **Grum botnet**, also known by its alias **Tedroo** and **Reddyb**, was a botnet mostly involved in sending pharmaceutical spam e-mails.[1] Once the world's largest botnet, Grum can be traced back to as early as 2008.[2] At the time of its shutdown in July 2012, Grum was reportedly the world's 3rd largest botnet,[3] responsible for 18% of worldwide spam traffic.[4][5]

Grum relies on two types of control servers for its operation. One type is used to push configuration updates to the infected computers, and the other is used to tell the botnet what spam emails to send.[6]

In July 2010, the Grum botnet consisted of an estimated 560,000–840,000 computers infected with the Grum rootkit.[7][8] The botnet alone delivered about 39.9 billion[9] spam messages in March 2010, equating to approximately 26% of the total global spam volume, temporarily making it the world's then-largest botnet.[10][11] Late in 2010, the botnet seemed to be growing, as its output increased roughly by 51% in comparison to its output in 2009 and early 2010. [12][13]

It used a panel written in PHP to control the botnet. [14]

18.1 Botnet takedown

In July 2012, malware intelligence company FireEye published an analysis of the botnet's command and control servers located in the Netherlands, Panama, and Russia. One week following their initial analysis, FireEye researchers reported that the Dutch Colo/ISP soon after seized two secondary servers responsible for sending spam instructions after their existence was made public.[15] Within one day, the Panamanian ISP hosting one of Grum's primary servers followed suit and shut down their server.[16] The cybercriminals behind Grum quickly responded by sending instructions through six newly established servers in Ukraine.[17] FireEye connected with Spamhaus, CERT-GIB, and an anonymous researcher to shut down the remaining six C&C servers, officially knocking down the bot-

net as of July 19, 2012.[17]

18.2 Grum botnet zombie clean-up

There was a sinkhole running on some of the former IP addresses of the Grumbot C&C servers. A feed from the sinkhole was processed via both Shadowserver and abusix to inform the Point of Contact at an ISP that has an infected IP addresses. ISP's are asked to contact their customers about the infections to have the malware cleaned up. Shadowserver.org will inform the users of their service once per day and Abusix sends out a X-ARF (extended version Abuse Reporting Format) report every hour.

18.3 See also

- Botnet
- Malware
- E-mail spam
- Internet crime
- Internet security

18.4 References

[1] "Grum". M86 Security. 2009-04-20. Retrieved 2010-07-30.

[2] Atif Mushtaq (2012-07-09). "Killing the Beast - Part 5". FireEye. Retrieved 2012-07-11.

[3] Mushtaq, Atif (2012-07-18). "Grum, World's Third-Largest Botnet, Knocked Down I FireEye Blog". Fireeye.com. Retrieved 2014-01-09.

[4] "Huge spam botnet Grum is taken out by security researchers". *BBC News*. 19 July 2012.

[5] "Researchers Say They Took Down World's Third-Largest Botnet". New York Times. 2012-07-18. Retrieved 2012-07-18.

[6] "One of the world's largest spam botnets still alive after suffering significant blow". IDG. 2012-07-17. Retrieved 2012-07-17.

[7] "Research: Small DIY botnets prevalent in enterprise networks". ZDNet. Retrieved 2010-07-30.

[8] "MessageLabs Blog - Evaluating Botnet Capacity". Messagelabs.com.sg. Retrieved 2010-07-30.

[9] "Which Botnet Is Worst? Report Offers New Perspective On Spam Growth - botnets/Security". DarkReading. Retrieved 2010-07-30.

[10] "Grum and Rustock botnets drive spam to new levels". Securecomputing.net.au. 2010-03-02. Retrieved 2010-07-30.

[11] Whitney, Lance (2010-03-02). "Botnets cause surge in February spam | Security - CNET News". News.cnet.com. Retrieved 2010-07-30.

[12] James Wray and Ulf Stabe (2010-03-01). "Spam volumes surge thanks Grum and Rustock botnets - Security". Thetechherald.com. Retrieved 2010-07-30.

[13] "MessageLabs: Botnets a threat to email marketing - Email Marketing". BizReport. 2009-09-30. Retrieved 2010-07-30.

[14] Brian Krebs (2012-08-20). "Inside the Grum botnet".

[15] Steve Ragan (2012-07-17). "Dutch Police Takedown C&Cs Used by Grum Botnet". Security Week. Retrieved 2012-07-17.

[16] Alex Fitzgerald (2012-07-19). "Botnet Responsible for 18% of World's Spam Knocked Offline". Mashable. Retrieved 2012-07-19.

[17] Atif Mushtaq (2012-07-19). "Grum, World's Third-Largest Botnet, Knocked Down". FireEye. Retrieved 2012-07-19.

Chapter 19

Gumblar

Gumblar is a malicious JavaScript trojan horse file that redirects a user's Google searches, and then installs rogue security software. Also known as **Troj/JSRedir-R**[1] this botnet first appeared in 2009.

19.1 Infection

19.1.1 Windows Personal Computers

Gumblar.X infections were widely seen on systems running older Windows operating systems.[2] Visitors to an infected site will be redirected to an alternative site containing further malware. Initially, this alternative site was gumblar.cn, but it has since switched to a variety of domains. The site sends the visitor an infected PDF that is opened by the visitor's browser or Acrobat Reader. The PDF will then exploit a known vulnerability in Acrobat to gain access to the user's computer. Newer variations of Gumblar redirect users to sites running fake anti-virus software.

The virus will find FTP clients such as FileZilla and Dreamweaver and download the clients' stored passwords. Gumblar also enables promiscuous mode on the network card, allowing it to sniff local network traffic for FTP details. It is one of the first viruses to incorporate an automated network sniffer.

19.1.2 Servers

Using passwords obtained from site admins, the host site will access a website via FTP and infect that website. It will download large portions of the website and inject malicious code into the website's files before uploading the files back onto the server. The code is inserted in any file that contains a **<body>** tag, such as HTML, PHP, JavaScript, ASP and ASPx files. The inserted PHP code contains base64-encoded JavaScript that will infect computers that execute the code. In addition, some pages may have inline frames inserted into them. Typically, iframe code contains hidden links to malicious websites.

The virus will also modify .htaccess and HOSTS files, and create images.php files in directories named 'images'. The infection is not a server-wide exploit. It will only infect sites on the server that it has passwords to.

19.2 Gumblar variants

Different companies use different names for Gumblar and variants. Initially, the malware was connecting to gumblar.cn domain but this server was shut down in May 2009.[3] However, many badware variants have emerged after that and they connect to other malicious servers via iframe code.

Gumblar resurfaced in January 2010, stealing FTP usernames and passwords and infecting HTML, PHP and JavaScript files on webservers to help spread itself.[4] This time it used multiple domains, making it harder to detect/stop.[5]

19.3 See also

- Malware
- E-mail spam
- Internet crime

19.4 References

[1] Matthew Broersma. "'Gumblar' attacks spreading quickly". Retrieved 26 July 2012.

[2] http://www.f-secure.com/v-descs/trojan-downloader_js_gumblar_x.shtml

[3] Binning, David (15 May 2009). "Reports of Gumblar's death greatly exaggerated". *Computer Weekly*. Retrieved 2009-07-07.

[4] "Gumblar-family virus removal tool".

[5] "Sucuri MW:JS:151 Gumblar malware - domains used".

19.5 External links

- Staff (15 May 2009). "New computer virus on rise, warn security experts". *The Telegraph (London)*. Retrieved 2009-07-07.

- Leyden, John (19 May 2009). "Gumblar Google-poisoning attack morphs". *The Register*. Retrieved 2009-07-07.

Chapter 20

Kelihos botnet

The **Kelihos botnet**, also known as **Hlux**, is a botnet mainly involved in spamming and the theft of bitcoins.[1]

20.1 History

The Kelihos botnet was first discovered around December 2010.[2] Researchers originally suspected having found a new version of either the Storm or Waledac botnet, due to similarities in the modus operandi and source code of the bot,[3][4] but analysis of the botnet showed it was instead a new, 45,000-infected-computer-strong, botnet that was capable of sending an estimated 4 billion spam messages a day.[5][6] In September 2011[7] Microsoft took down the botnet in an operation codenamed "Operation b79".[5][8] At the same time, Microsoft filed civil charges against Dominique Alexander Piatti, dotFREE Group SRO and 22 John Doe defendants for suspected involvement in the botnet for issuing 3,700 subdomains that were used by the botnet.[8][9] These charges were later dropped when Microsoft determined that the named defendants did not intentionally aid the botnet controllers.[10][11]

In January 2012 a new version of the botnet was discovered, one sometimes referred to as Kelihos.b or Version 2,[1][6][7] consisting of an estimated 110,000 infected computers.[1][12] During this same month Microsoft pressed charges against Russian citizen Andrey Sabelnikov, a former IT security professional, for being the alleged creator of the Kelihos Botnet sourcecode.[11][13][14] The second version of the botnet itself was shut down by it in March 2012 by several privately owned firms by sinkholing it – a technique which gave the companies control over the botnet while cutting off the original controllers.[2][15]

Following the shutdown of the second version of the botnet, a new version surfaced as early as 2 April, though there is some disagreement between research groups whether the botnet is simply the remnants of the disabled Version 2 botnet, or a new version altogether.[16][17] This version of the botnet currently consists of an estimated 70,000 infected computers. The Kelihos.c version mostly infects computers through Facebook by sending users of the website malicious download links. Once clicked, a Trojan horse named Fifesoc is downloaded, which turns the computer into a zombie, which is part of the botnet.[18]

On 24 November 2015 a Kelihos botnet event occurred causing widespread false positives of blacklisted IPs:

"November 24, 2015 Widespread false positives

Earlier today, a very large scale Kelihos botnet event occurred - by large scale, many email installations will be seeing in excess of 20% kelihos spam, and some will see their inbound email volume jump by a volume of as much as 500%. This isn't an unusual thing normally, the CBL/XBL has been successfully dealing with large scale Kelihos spam spikes like this, often daily, for years.

The email was allegedly from the US Federal Reserve, saying something about restrictions in "U.S. Federal Wire and ACH online payments." Not only was the notice itself fraudulent, the attached Excel spreadsheet (.xls) contained macro instructions (a downloader) to download a Windows executable virus, most likely Dyreza or Dridex malware.

The detection rules initially deployed by the CBL unfortunately were insufficiently detailed, and listed a number of IP addresses in error." [19]

20.2 Structure, operations and spread

The Kelihos botnet is a so-called peer-to-peer botnet, where individual botnet nodes are capable of acting as command-and-control servers for the entire botnet. In traditional non-peer-to-peer botnets, all the nodes receive their instructions and "work" from a limited set of servers – if these servers are removed or taken down, the botnet will no longer receive instructions and will therefore effectively shut down.[20] Peer-to-peer botnets seek to mitigate that risk by allowing every peer to send instructions to the entire botnet, thus making it more difficult to shut it down.[2]

The first version of the botnet was mainly involved in denial-of-service attacks and email spam, while version two of the botnet added the ability to steal Bitcoin wallets, as well as a program used to mine bitcoins itself.[2][21] Its spam capacity allows the botnet to spread itself by sending malware links to users in order to infect them with a Trojan horse, though later versions mostly propagate over social network sites, in particular through Facebook.[16][22]

20.3 See also

- Botnet

- Malware

- E-mail spam

- Internet crime

- Internet security

20.4 References

[1] Mills, Elinor (28 March 2012). "110,000 PC-strong Kelihos botnet sidelined". *CNET*. Retrieved 28 April 2012.

[2] Ortloff, Stefan (28 March 2012). "FAQ: Disabling the new Hlux/Kelihos Botnet". *Securelist.com*. Retrieved 28 April 2012.

[3] Adair, Steven (30 December 2010). "New Fast Flux Botnet for the Holidays: Could it be Storm Worm 3.0/Waledac 2.0?". *Shadowserver*. Retrieved 28 April 2012.

[4] Donohue, Brian (29 March 2012). "Kelihos Returns: Same Botnet or New Version?". *Threatpost*. Retrieved 28 April 2012.

[5] Mills, Elinor (27 September 2011). "Microsoft halts another botnet: Kelihos". *CNet*. Retrieved 28 April 2012.

[6] Kirk, Jeremy (1 February 2012). "Kelihos botnet, once crippled, now gaining strength". *Network World*. Retrieved 28 April 2012.

[7] Constantin, Lucian (28 March 2012). "Security Firms Disable the Second Kelihos Botnet". *PCWorld*. Retrieved 28 April 2012.

[8] Boscovich, Richard (27 September 2011). "Microsoft Neutralizes Kelihos Botnet, Names Defendant in Case". *Microsoft TechNet*. Retrieved 28 April 2012.

[9] Microsoft (26 September 2011). "Operation b79 (Kelihos) and Additional MSRT September Release". *Microsoft Technet*. Retrieved 28 April 2012.

[10] Latif, Lawrence (27 October 2011). "Microsoft drops Kelihos botnet allegations against ISP owner". *The Inquirer*. Retrieved 28 April 2012.

[11] Gonsalves, Antone (24 January 2012). "Microsoft Says Ex-Antivirus Maker Ran Botnet". *CRN Magazine*. Retrieved 28 April 2012.

[12] Warren, Tom (29 March 2012). "Second Kelihos botnet downed, 116,000 machines freed". *The Verge*. Retrieved 28 April 2012.

[13] Brewster, Tom (24 January 2012). "Microsoft suspects ex-antivirus worker of Kelihos botnet creation". *IT PRO*. Retrieved 28 April 2012.

[14] Keizer, Gregg (24 January 2012). "Accused Kelihos botnet maker worked for two security firms | ITworld". *ITworld*. Retrieved 28 April 2012.

[15] Donohue, Brian (28 March 2012). "Kaspersky Knocks Down Kelihos Botnet Again, But Expects Return". *ThreatPost*. Retrieved 28 April 2012.

[16] Raywood, Dan (2 April 2012). "CrowdStrike researchers deny that Kelihos has spawned a new version – SC Magazine UK". *SC Magazine*. Retrieved 29 April 2012.

[17] Leyden, John (29 March 2012). "Kelihos zombies erupt from mass graves after botnet massacre". *The Register*. Retrieved 28 April 2012.

[18] SPAMfighter News, (13 April 2012). "Kelihos Botnet Re-emerges, This Time Attacking Social Networks". *SPAMfighter*. Retrieved 28 April 2012.

[19] http://www.abuseat.org

[20] Grizzard, Julian; David Dagon; Vikram Sharma; Chris Nunnery; Brent ByungHoon Kang (3 April 2007). "Peer-to-Peer Botnets: Overview and Case Study". *The Johns Hopkins University Applied Physics Laboratory*. Retrieved 28 April 2012.

[21] SPAMfighter (5 April 2012). "Security Companies Take Down Kelihos Botnet of Version 2". *SPAMfighter*. Retrieved 28 April 2012.

[22] Jorgenson, Petra (6 April 2012). "Kelihos Botnet Could Resurge via Facebook Worm". *Midsize Insider*. Retrieved 29 April 2012.

Chapter 21

Kraken botnet

The **Kraken botnet** was the world's largest botnet as of April 2008. Researchers say that Kraken infected machines in at least 50 of the Fortune 500 companies and grew to over 400,000 bots.[1] It was estimated to send 9 billion spam messages per day. Kraken botnet malware may have been designed to evade anti-virus software, and employed techniques to stymie conventional anti-virus software.[2]

In April 2008, Damballa released instructions for removing Kraken malware from computers and a list of IPs that are part of the Kraken botnet. The list shows that on April 13, 2008, there were 495,000 computers in the Kraken botnet.

21.1   See also

- Computer worm

- Internet bot

21.2   References

[1] Higgins, Kelly Jackson (7 April 2008). "New Massive Botnet Twice the Size of Storm". *Dark Reading.* Retrieved 7 April 2008.

[2] Goodin, Dan (7 April 2008). "Move over Storm – there's a bigger, stealthier botnet in town". *The Register.* Retrieved 7 April 2008.

21.3   External links

- Fisher, Dennis, Kraken botnet balloons to dangerous levels, SearchSecurity.com, Apr. 7, 2008, retrieved 2008-04-07

- Orion, Egan, There's a new botnet worm on the loose: Kraken seeks to sink the Fortune 500, *The Inquirer*, April 7, 2008, retrieved 2008-04-07

- Neri, Kraken Botnet, la Botnet mas grande del Mundo, retrieved 2008-04-07, en español.

- Pierce, Cody, Owning Kraken Zombies, a Detailed Dissection, 2008-04-28, retrieved 2008-04-28

- Amini, Pedram, Kraken Botnet Infiltration, 2008-04-28, retrieved 2008-04-28

Chapter 22

Lethic botnet

The **Lethic Botnet** (initially discovered around 2008[1]) is a botnet consisting of an estimated 210 000 - 310 000 individual machines [2] which are mainly involved in pharmaceutical and replica spam.[3] At the peak of its existence the botnet was responsible for 8-10% of all the spam sent worldwide.[1]

22.1 Dismantling and revival

Around early January 2010 the botnet was dismantled by Neustar employees, who contacted various Lethic internet service providers in a bid to take control of the botnet's command and control servers.[4][5][6][7] This move temporarily caused the botnets' spam to decrease to a trickle of its original volume.[8]

In February 2010 the owners of the botnet managed to re-establish control over the botnet, through the use of new command and control servers located in the United States. The takedown has decreased the spam volume of the botnet, however. As of February 2010 the botnets' amount of spam was down to a third of its original.[3] As of April 2010 the botnet has an estimated 1.5% share of the spam market, sending about 2 billion spam messages a day.[2]

22.2 See also

- Botnet

- Malware

- Internet crime

- Internet security

- Command and control (malware)

- Zombie (computer science)

22.3 References

[1] "Lethic". M86 Security. 2010-01-06. Retrieved 2010-08-28.

[2] "Symantec.cloud | Email Security, Web Security, Endpoint Protection, Archiving, Continuity, Instant Messaging Security" (PDF). Messagelabs.com. 2010-04-04. Retrieved 2014-01-09.

[3] "Lethic is Back in the Game". M86 Security. Retrieved 2010-08-28.

[4] Leyden, John (2010-02-17). "Undead botnets blamed for big rise in email malware; Grave concern over reanimated cyber-corpses". *theregister.co.uk*. London, UK: The Register. Retrieved 2014-01-09.

[5] Leyden, John (2010-01-13). "Lethic botnet knocked out by security researchers; Zombie network taken down". *theregister.co.uk*. London, UK: The Register. Retrieved 2014-01-09.

[6] "More Researchers Going On The Offensive To Kill Botnets". DarkReading. Retrieved 2010-08-28.

[7] "Spammers survive botnet shutdowns". BBC News. 2010-03-18. Retrieved 2010-08-28.

[8] "Lethic botnet - The Takedown". M86 Security. Retrieved 2010-08-28.

22.4 External links

- Technical analysis of the Lethic botnet

Chapter 23

Mariposa botnet

The **Mariposa botnet**, discovered December 2008,[1] is a botnet mainly involved in cyberscamming and denial-of-service attacks.[2][3] Before the botnet itself was dismantled on 23 December 2009, it consisted of up to 12 million unique IP addresses or up to 1 million individual zombie computers infected with the "Butterfly (*mariposa* in Spanish) Bot", making it one of the largest known botnets.[3][4][5]

23.1 History

23.1.1 Origins and initial spread

The botnet was originally created by the DDP Team (Spanish: *Días de Pesadilla Team*, English: *Nightmare Days Team*), using a malware program called "Butterfly bot", which was also sold to various individuals and organisations.[2][6] The goal of this malware program was to install itself on an uninfected PC, monitoring activity for passwords, bank credentials and credit cards.[2] After that the malware would attempt to self-propagate to other connectible systems using various supported methods, such as MSN, P2P and USB.[7]

After completing its initial infection routine the malware would contact a command-and-control server within the botnet. This command and control server could be used by the controllers of the botnet, in order to issue orders to the botnet itself.[8]

23.1.2 Operations and impact

The operations executed by the botnet were diverse, in part because parts of the botnet could be rented by third party individuals and organizations.[9] Confirmed activities include denial-of-service attacks, e-mail spam, theft of personal information, and changing the search results a browser would display in order to show advertisements and pop-up ads.[8][10]

Due to the size and nature of a botnet its total financial and social impact is difficult to calculate, but initial estimates calculated that the removal of the malware alone could cost "tens of millions of dollars".[8][11] After the apprehension of the botnet's operators government officials also discovered a list containing personal details on 800,000 individuals, which could be used or sold for Identity theft purposes.[11]

23.1.3 Dismantling

In May 2009 the Mariposa Working Group (MWG) was formed as an informal group, composed of Defence Intelligence (company), the Georgia Tech Information Security Center and Panda Security, along with additional unnamed security researchers and law enforcement agencies. The goal of this group was the analysis and extermination of the Mariposa botnet itself.[8]

On 23 December 2009 the Mariposa Working Group managed to take control of the Mariposa Botnet, after seizing control of the command-and-control servers used by the botnet. The operational owners of the botnet eventually succeeded in regaining control over the botnet, and in response launched a denial-of-service attack on Defence Intelligence.[8] The attack itself managed to knock out Internet connectivity for a large share of the ISP's customers, which included several Canadian universities and government agencies.[12]

On 3 February 2010, the Spanish national police arrested Florencio Carro Ruiz (alias: Netkairo) as the suspected leader of the DDP Team. Two additional arrests were made on 24 February 2010. Jonathan Pazos Rivera (alias: Jonyloleante) and Juan Jose Bellido Rios (alias: Ostiator) were arrested on the suspicion of being members of DDP.[3][8][13][14][15]

On 18 July 2010, Matjaž Škorjanc (alias: Iserdo), the creator of the "Butterfly bot" malware, was arrested in Maribor by Slovenian police for the first time,[16] but released due to lack of evidence. He was arrested again in October 2011.[17] In December 2013 Škorjanc was convicted in

Slovenia of "creating a malicious computer program for hacking information systems, assisting in wrongdoings and money laundering."[18] He was sentenced to 4 years and 10 months imprisonment and fined €3,000 ($4,100).[19] The court also ordered the seizure of Škorjanc's property acquired with the proceeds of crime.[20] After he appealed the verdict his fine was in February 2015 raised for additional 25,000 EUR.[21]

23.2 References

[1] "FBI arrests 'mastermind' of Mariposa botnet computer code". *The Daily Telegraph*. London. 28 July 2010. Retrieved 29 July 2010.

[2] Zerdin, Ali (28 July 2010). "Cyber mastermind arrested, questioned in Slovenia". *The Washington Times*. Washington, D.C. Retrieved 29 July 2010.

[3] "Suspected 'Mariposa Botnet' creator arrested". *canada.com*. 28 July 2010. Archived from the original on May 11, 2011. Retrieved 29 July 2010.

[4] Thompson, Matt (7 October 2009). "Mariposa Botnet Analysis" (PDF). *Defintel*. Retrieved 29 July 2010.

[5] Krebs, Brian. "Accused Mariposa Botnet Operators Sought Jobs at Spanish Security Firm". Retrieved 14 October 2014.

[6] "FBI says cyber mastermind nabbed". *The New Zealand Herald*. 28 July 2010. Retrieved 29 July 2010.

[7] Coogan, Peter (7 October 2009). "The Mariposa/Butterfly Bot Kit". *Symantec*. Retrieved 29 July 2010.

[8] Corrons, Luis (3 March 2010). "Mariposa botnet". *Panda Security*. Retrieved 29 July 2010.

[9] "Massive Mariposa botnet shut down". *Help Net Security*. 3 March 2010. Retrieved 29 July 2010.

[10] Krebs, Brian (4 March 2010). "'Mariposa' Botnet Authors May Avoid Jail Time". *Krebs on Security*. Retrieved 29 July 2010.

[11] "Spain busts ring accused of infecting 13 mln PCs". Reuters. 2010-03-02. Retrieved 2010-07-29.

[12] Larraz, Teresa (3 March 2010). "UPDATE 1-Spain busts ring accused of infecting 13 mln PCs". *Reuters*. Retrieved 29 July 2010.

[13] Ragan, Steve (3 March 2010). "Mariposa botnet – 12.7 million bots strong – knocked offline". *The Tech Herald*. Retrieved 29 July 2010.

[14] "Cyber mastermind arrested, questioned in Slovenia". *WTOP-FM*. Retrieved 29 July 2010.

[15] "FBI, Slovenian and Spanish Police Arrest Mariposa Botnet Creator, Operators". *FBI National Press Office*. Washington, D.C. 28 July 2010. Retrieved 27 December 2013.

[16] "FBI potrdil aretacijo štajerskega hekerja; ta že na prostosti" [FBI Confirms the Arrest of the Styrian Hacker; He Is Already at Large] (in Slovenian). 28 July 2010.

[17] "Afera Mariposa: Škorjanc se ni želel zagovarjati" [Mariposa Affair: Škorjanc Refuses to Defend Himself]. *Delo.si* (in Slovenian). 6 August 2012.

[18] "Creator of Mariposa Botnet Sentenced to 58 Months in Prison". *Security Week*. 23 December 2013. Retrieved 27 December 2013.

[19] "Hacker sentenced for 'malicious' programme". *IOL*. 24 December 2013. Retrieved 27 December 2013.

[20] "Mariposa botnet 'mastermind' jailed in Slovenia". *BBC News*. 24 December 2013. Retrieved 27 December 2013.

[21] "Mariposa Botnet Hacker Fails with Appeal at Higher Court". Slovenian Press Agency. 5 February 2015.

23.3 External links

- Analysis of the Mariposa botnet

Chapter 24

Mega-D botnet

The **Mega-D**, also known by its alias of **Ozdok**, is a botnet that at its peak was responsible for sending 32% of spam worldwide.[1][2][3]

On October 14, 2008, the U.S Federal Trade Commission, in cooperation with Marshal Software, tracked down the owners of the botnet and froze their assets.[4]

On November 6, 2009, security company FireEye, Inc. disabled the Mega-D botnet by disabling its command and control structure.[5][6] This was akin to the Srizbi botnet takedown in late 2008. The Mega-D/Ozdok takedown involved coordination of dozens of Internet service providers, domain name registrars, and non-profit organizations like Shadowserver. M86 Security researchers estimated the take down had an immediate effect on the spam from the botnet. On November 9, 2009, the spam had stopped altogether, although there was a very small trickle over the weekend, directed to a couple of small UK-based domains that they monitored.[7]

Since then the botnet bounced back, exceeding pre-takedown levels by Nov. 22, and constituting 17% of worldwide spam by Dec. 13.[8]

In July 2010, researchers from University of California, Berkeley published a model of Mega-D's protocol state-machine, revealing the internals of the proprietary protocol for the first time.[9] The protocol was obtained through automatic Reverse Engineering technique developed by the Berkeley researchers. Among other contributions, their research paper reveals a flaw in the Mega-D protocol allowing template milking, i.e., unauthorized spam template downloading. Such a flaw could be used to acquire spam templates and train spam filters before spam hits the network.

24.1 Arrest

Main article: Oleg Nikolaenko

In November 2010, Oleg Nikolaenko was arrested in Las Vegas, Nevada by the Federal Bureau of Investigation and charged with violations of the CAN-SPAM Act of 2003.[10] Nikolaenko is suspected of operating the Mega-D botnet to create a "zombie network" of as many as 500,000 infected computers.[11]

24.2 See also

- Storm botnet
- MPack malware kit
- E-mail spam
- Internet crime
- Internet security
- Operation: Bot Roast
- McColo
- Srizbi

24.3 References

[1] "Storm worm dethroned by sex botnet". Networkworld.com. Retrieved 2010-07-31.

[2] "New Mega-D botnet supersedes Storm". SPAMfighter. 2008-02-01. Retrieved 2010-07-31.

[3] "New Mega-D menace muscles Storm Worm aside". ars technica. February 2008. Retrieved 2011-12-06.

[4] Stone, Brad (October 14, 2008). "Authorities Shut Down Spam Ring". *The New York Times*.

[5] Smashing the Mega-d/Ozdok botnet in 24 hours

[6] Cheng, Jacqui (November 11, 2009). "Researchers' well-aimed stone takes down Goliath botnet". Ars Technica. Retrieved 2009-11-30.

[7] "Mega-D botnet takes a hit". M86 Security. November 9, 2009. Retrieved 2009-11-30.

[8] "Spam Statisti cs from the Security Labs team at M86 Security". M86 Security. Retrieved 2010-06-07.

[9] C.Y. Cho, D. Babic, R. Shin, and D. Song. Inference and Analysis of Formal Models of Botnet Command and Control Protocols, 2010 ACM Conference on Computer and Communications Security.

[10] Vielmetti, Bruce (December 3, 2010). "Milwaukee FBI agent trips up Russian 'king of spam'". *Milwaukee Journal Sentinel*. Retrieved December 3, 2010.

[11] Leyden, John (December 1, 2010). "Feds pursue Russian, 23, behind ⅓ of ALL WORLD SPAM". *The Register*. Retrieved December 3, 2010.

Chapter 25

Metulji botnet

The **Metulji botnet**, discovered in June 2011,[1] is a botnet mainly involved in cyberscamming and denial of service attacks. Before the botnet itself was dismantled, it consisted of over 12 million individual zombie computers infected with the "Butterfly Bot", making it, as of June 2011, the largest known botnet.[1]

It is not known what type of computers are vulnerable, or how to tell if a computer is a part of this botnet.

25.1   See also

- Carna botnet

- Command and control (malware)

- Computer worm

- Spambot

- Timeline of notable computer viruses and worms

- Xor DDoS

- Zombie (computer science)

- ZeroAccess botnet

25.2   Notes

[1] Clayton, Mark (30 June 2011) "How the FBI and Interpol trapped the world's biggest Butterfly botnet", *Christian Science Monitor*

Chapter 26

Mevade Botnet

The **Mevade Botnet**, also known as **Sefnit** or **SBC**, is a massive botnet. Its operators are unknown and its motives seems to be multi-purpose.[1]

In late 2013 the Tor anonymity network saw a very sudden and significant increase in users, from 800,000 daily to more than 5,000,000. A botnet was suspected and fingers pointed at Mevade. Trend Micro reported that it's Smart Protection Network saw a tor module being distributed to Mevade Trojans.[2]

26.1 See also

- Conficker

- Command and control (malware)

- Gameover ZeuS

- Operation Tovar

- Timeline of computer viruses and worms

- Tiny Banker Trojan

- Torpig

- Zeus (malware)

- Zombie (computer science)

26.2 References

[1] Debbie Cohen-Abravanel (November 6, 2013). "Mevade Botnet Attacking Enterprises & Governments".

[2] "Massive spike of Tor users caused by Mevade botnet".

Chapter 27

Mirai (malware)

Mirai is a piece of Malware perhaps best known for launching one of the largest distributed denial-of-service attacks.[1]

Mirai was brought into the spotlight after being used to launch a distributed denial of service attack on Brian Krebs website krebsonsecurity.com which reached 620 Gbps and is considered the largest if not the largest denial of service attack.[2]

Mirai functions by infecting IoT devices by trying to brute force their passwords.[3] The tactic it uses to brute force passwords is entering commonly used and default passwords.[4][5] Several things have been noted in Mirai.[6] Such as the bots being written in C and the Command & control being written in Go and the fact it contains a list of IPs for which to avoid activating it's scans on.[7]

After attracting attention from the security community due to the massive DDoS attacks, the author of Mirai decided to release the source code of Mirai.[8][9][10][11]

27.1 See also

- Low Orbit Ion Cannon A stress test tool that has been used for DDoS attacks

- High Orbit Ion Cannon The replacement for LOIC used in DDoS attacks

- Fork bomb

- Denial-of-service attack

- Slowloris (computer security)

- ReDoS

27.2 References

[1] Hackett, Robert (October 3, 2016). "Why a Hacker Dumped Code Behind Colossal Website-Trampling Botnet". Fortune.com. Retrieved 19 October 2016.

[2] Biggs, John (Oct 10, 2016). "Hackers release source code for a powerful DDoS app called Mirai". TechCrunch. Retrieved 19 October 2016.

[3] Kan, Michael (Oct 18, 2016). "Hackers create more IoT botnets with Mirai source code". Computerworld. Retrieved 20 October 2016.

[4] Bonderud, Douglas (October 4, 2016). "Leaked Mirai Malware Boosts IoT Insecurity Threat Level". securityintelligence.com. Retrieved 20 October 2016.

[5] Osborne, Charlie (October 17, 2016). "Mirai DDoS botnet powers up, infects Sierra Wireless gateways". ZDNet. Retrieved 20 October 2016.

[6] Moffitt, Tyler (October 10, 2016). "Source Code for Mirai IoT Malware Released". Webroot. Retrieved 20 October 2016.

[7] Zeifman, Igal; Bekerman, Dima; Herzberg, Ben (October 10, 2016). "Breaking Down Mirai: An IoT DDoS Botnet Analysis". Incapsula. Retrieved 20 October 2016.

[8] Cimpanu, Catalin (Oct 19, 2016). "There Are Almost Half a Million IoT Devices Infected with the Mirai IoT Malware". Softpedia. Retrieved 20 October 2016.

[9] Goodin, Dan (Oct 2, 2016). "Brace yourselves—source code powering potent IoT DDoSes just went public". Ars Technica. Retrieved 20 October 2016.

[10] Kan, Michael (October 18, 2016). "Hackers create more IoT botnets with Mirai source code". ITWORLD. Retrieved 20 October 2016.

[11] Mimoso, Michael (October 3, 2016). "Source Code Released for Mirai DDoS Malware". threatpost.com. Retrieved 20 October 2016.

Chapter 28

Necurs botnet

The **Necurs botnet** is a distributor of many pieces of malware, most notably Locky.

28.1 Reports

Around June 1, 2016, the botnet went offline, perhaps due to a glitch in the command and control server. However, three weeks later, Jon French from AppRiver discovered a spike in spam emails, signifying either a temporary spike in the botnet's activity or return to its normal pre-June 1 state.[1]

28.2 Distributed Malware[2]

- Bart

- Dridex

- Locky

- RockLoader

28.3 See also

- Conficker

- Command and control (malware)

- Gameover ZeuS

- Operation Tovar

- Timeline of computer viruses and worms

- Tiny Banker Trojan

- Torpig

- Zeus (malware)

- Zombie (computer science)

28.4 References

[1] French, Jon. "Necurs BotNet Back With A Vengeance Warns AppRiver". Retrieved 27 June 2016.

[2] "Hackers behind Locky and Dridex start spreading new ransomware". Retrieved 27 June 2016.

Chapter 29

Nitol botnet

The **Nitol botnet** mostly involved in spreading malware and distributed denial-of-service attacks.[1][2]

29.1 History

The Nitol Botnet was first discovered around December 2012, with analysis of the botnet indicating that the botnet is mostly prevalent in China where an estimate 85% of the infections are detected.[3][4] In China the botnet was found to be present on systems that came brand-new from the factory, indicating the trojan was installed somewhere during the assembly and manufacturing process.[5] According to Microsoft the systems at risk also contained a counterfeit installation of Microsoft Windows.[3]

On 10 September 2012 Microsoft took action against the Nitol Botnet by obtaining a court order and subsequently Sinkholing the 3322.org domain.[6][7] The 3322.org domain is a Dynamic DNS which was used by the botnet creators as a command and control infrastructure for controlling their botnet.[8] Microsoft later settled with 3322.org operator Pen Yong, which allowed the latter to continue operating the domain on the condition that any subdomains linked to malware remain sinkholed.[9]

29.2 See also

- Internet crime

- Internet security

29.3 References

[1] Gonsalves, Antone. "Compromised Windows PCs bought in China pose risk to U.S.". Networkworld. Retrieved 27 December 2012.

[2] Plantado, Rex (15 Oct 2012). "MSRT October '12 - Nitol: Counterfeit code isn't such a great deal after all". *Microsoft*. Microsoft Technet. Retrieved 27 December 2012.

[3] Plantado, Rex (22 Oct 2012). "MSRT October '12 - Nitol by the numbers". *Microsoft*. Microsoft Technet. Retrieved 27 December 2012.

[4] Mimoso, Michael (September 13, 2012). "Microsoft Carries out Nitol Botnet Takedown". Threatpost. Retrieved 27 December 2012.

[5] "Microsoft Report Exposes Malware Families Attacking Supply Chain". BBC. Retrieved 27 December 2012.

[6] Leyden, John (13 September 2012). "Microsoft seizes Chinese dot-org to kill Nitol bot army". *The Register*. Retrieved 27 December 2012.

[7] Jackson Higgins, Kelly (Sep 13, 2012). "Microsoft Intercepts 'Nitol' Botnet And 70,000 Malicious Domains". Dark Reading. Retrieved 27 December 2012.

[8] Ollmann, Gunter (September 13, 2012). "Nitol and 3322.org Takedown by Microsoft". Damballa. Retrieved 27 December 2012.

[9] Leyden, John (4 October 2012). "Chinese Nitol botnet host back up after Microsoft settles lawsuit". *The Register*. Retrieved 27 December 2012.

29.4 External links

- Analysis of the Nitol Botnet, created by Microsoft as part of Operation b70

Chapter 30

Operation: Bot Roast

Operation: Bot Roast is an operation by the FBI to track down bot herders, crackers, or virus coders who install malicious software on computers through the Internet without the owners' knowledge, which turns the computer into a zombie computer that then sends out spam to other computers from the compromised computer, making a botnet or network of bot infected computers. The operation was launched because the vast scale of botnet resources poses a threat to national security.[1]

30.1 The results

The operation was created to disrupt and disassemble bot herders. In June 2007, the FBI had identified about 1 million computers that were compromised, leading to the arrest of the persons responsible for creating the malware. In the process, owners of infected computers were notified, many of whom were unaware of the exploitation.[1][2]

Some early results of the operation include charges against the following:

- Robert Alan Soloway of Seattle, Washington, pleaded guilty to charges of using botnets to send tens of millions of spam messages touting his website.[1]

- Jeanson James Ancheta plead guilty to controlling thousands of infected computers.[3]

- Jason Michael Downey (pseudonym "Nessun"), founder of the IRC network Rizon, is charged with using botnets to disable other systems.[1]

- Akbot author Owen Walker (pseudonym "AKILL") of New Zealand, was tried for various crimes and discharged by the prosecution in 2008.[4]

30.2 See also

- Botnet

- E-mail spam
- Internet crime
- Internet security
- Storm botnet
- Lycos Europe

30.3 References

[1] "OPERATION: BOT ROAST 'Bot-herders' Charged as Part of Initiative" (Press release). Federal Bureau of Investigation. 2007-06-13. Retrieved 2012-11-26.

[2] "FBI tries to fight zombie hordes" (Press release). BBC News. 2007-06-14. Retrieved 2007-06-20.

[3] Dan Goodin (13 June 2007). "FBI logs its millionth zombie address". the register. Retrieved 2008-09-26.

[4] Akill pleads guilty to all charges, By Ulrika Hedquist, 1 April 2008, Computerworld

Chapter 31

Rustock botnet

The **Rustock botnet** was a botnet that operated from around 2006[1] until March 2011.

It consisted of computers running Microsoft Windows, and was capable of sending up to 25,000 spam messages per hour from an infected PC.[2][3] At the height of its activities, it sent an average of 192 spam messages per compromised machine per minute.[4] Reported estimates on its size vary greatly across different sources, with claims that the botnet may have comprised anywhere between 150,000 and 2,400,000 machines.[5][6][7] The size of the botnet was increased and maintained mostly through self-propagation, where the botnet sent many malicious e-mails intended to infect machines opening them with a trojan which would incorporate the machine into the botnet.[8]

The botnet took a hit after the 2008 takedown of McColo, an ISP which was responsible for hosting most of the botnet's command and control servers. McColo regained internet connectivity for several hours and in those hours up to 15 Mbit a second of traffic was observed, likely indicating a transfer of command and control to Russia.[9] While these actions temporarily reduced global spam levels by around 75%, the effect did not last long: spam levels increased by 60% between January and June 2009, 40% of which was attributed to the Rustock botnet.[10][11]

On March 16, 2011, the botnet was taken down through what was initially reported as a coordinated effort by Internet service providers and software vendors.[12] It was revealed the next day that the take-down, called Operation b107,[13][14] was the action of Microsoft, U.S. federal law enforcement agents, FireEye, and the University of Washington.[15][16]

To capture the individuals involved with the Rustock botnet, on July 18, 2011, Microsoft is offering "a monetary reward in the amount of US$250,000 for new information that results in the identification, arrest and criminal conviction of such individual(s)."[17]

31.1 Operations

Botnets are composed of infected computers used by unwitting Internet users. In order to hide its presence from the user and anti-virus software the Rustock botnet employed rootkit technology. Once a computer was infected, it would seek contact with command-and-control servers at a number of IP addresses and any of 2,500 domains and backup domains[18] that may direct the zombies in the botnet to perform various tasks such as sending spam or executing distributed denial of service (DDoS) attacks.[19] Ninety-six servers were in operation at the time of the takedown.[20] When sending spam the botnet uses TLS encryption in around 35 percent of the cases as an extra layer of protection to hide its presence. Whether detected or not, this creates additional overhead for the mail servers handling the spam. Some experts pointed out that this extra load could negatively impact the mail infrastructure of the Internet, as most of the e-mails sent these days are spam.[21]

31.2 See also

- Botnet
- Helpful worm
- McColo
- Operation: Bot Roast
- Srizbi Botnet
- Command and control (malware)
- Zombie (computer science)
- Alureon
- Conficker
- Gameover ZeuS
- Storm botnet

- Bagle (computer worm)

- ZeroAccess botnet

- Regin (malware)

- Zeus (malware)

31.3   References

[1] Chuck Miller (2008-07-25). "The Rustock botnet spams again". SC Magazine US. Retrieved 2010-04-21.

[2] "Real Viagra sales power global spam flood - Techworld.com". News.techworld.com. Retrieved 2010-04-21.

[3] "Marshal8e6 Releases New Insight and Analysis into Botnets". *trustwave.com*. Chicago, IL, USA: Trustwave Holdings. 2009-04-22. Retrieved 2014-01-09.

[4] "Symantec Announces August 2010 MessageLabs Intelligence Report". *symantec.com*. Sunnyvale, CA, USA: Symantec. 2010-08-24. Retrieved 2014-01-09.

[5] "MessageLabs intelligence" (PDF). MessageLabs. April 2010. Retrieved 20 November 2010.

[6] "Biggest spammer? The Rustock botnet I". Securityinfowatch.com. 2009-02-06. Retrieved 2010-04-21.

[7] "Rustock botnet responsible for 40 percent of spam". Good Gear Guide. Retrieved August 25, 2010.

[8] "New Rustock Botnet Trying to Expand Itself". SPAMfighter. 2008-07-25. Retrieved 2010-04-21.

[9] "Dead network provider arms Rustock botnet from the hereafter - McColo dials Russia as world sleeps". The Register. 18 November 2008. Retrieved 20 November 2010.

[10] "Rustock botnet leads spam surge up 60 percent in 2009". MX Logic. 2009-07-14. Retrieved 2010-04-21.

[11] "Grum and Rustock botnets drive spam to new levels > Botnet > Vulnerabilities & Exploits > News > SC Magazine Australia/NZ". securecomputing.net.au. 2010-03-02. Retrieved 2010-04-21.

[12] Hickins, Michael (2011-03-17). "Prolific Spam Network Is Unplugged". Wall Street Journal. Retrieved 2011-03-17.

[13] Williams, Jeff. "Operation b107 - Rustock Botnet Takedown". Retrieved 2011-03-27.

[14] Bright, Peter. "How Operation b107 decapitated the Rustock botnet". Ars Technica. Retrieved 2011-03-27.

[15] Wingfield, Nick (2011-03-18). "Spam Network Shut Down". Wall Street Journal. Retrieved 2011-03-18.

[16] Williams, Jeff. "Operation b107 - Rustock Botnet Takedown". Retrieved 2011-04-06.

[17] "Microsoft Offers Reward for Information on Rustock". Retrieved 2011-07-18.

[18] Microsoft Amended Application for Temporary Restraining Order. Case 11CV00222, US Fed. Ct. W.D. Wash., Feb 28 2011

[19] Prince, Brian (2009-07-28). "Security: A Day in the Life of the Rustock Botnet". EWeek. Retrieved 20 November 2010.

[20] "Spammers sought after botnet takedown". *BBC News*. 2011-03-25.

[21] "Beware Botnet's Return, Security Firms Warn". PCWorld. 2010-03-28. Retrieved 2010-04-21.

Chapter 32

Sality

Sality is the classification for a family of malicious software (malware), which infects files on Microsoft Windows systems. Sality was first discovered in 2003 and has advanced over the years to become a dynamic, enduring and full-featured form of malicious code. Systems infected with Sality may communicate over a peer-to-peer (P2P) network for the purpose of relaying spam, proxying of communications, exfiltrating sensitive data, compromising web servers and/or coordinating distributed computing tasks for the purpose of processing intensive tasks (e.g. password cracking). Since 2010, certain variants of Sality have also incorporated the use of rootkit functions as part of an ongoing evolution of the malware family. Because of its continued development and capabilities, Sality is considered to be one of the most complex and formidable forms of malware to date.

32.1 Aliases

The majority of Antivirus (A/V) vendors use the following naming conventions when referring to this family of malware (the * at the end of the names is a wildcard for all the possible classifications and/or distinctions for this malware family):

- Sality
- SalLoad
- Kookoo
- SaliCode

32.2 Malware Profile

32.2.1 Summary

Sality is a family of polymorphic file infectors, which target Windows executable files with the extensions .EXE or .SCR.[1] Sality utilizes polymorphic and entry-point obscuring (EPO) techniques to infect files using the following methods: not changing the entry point address of the host, and replacing the original host code at the entry point of the executable with a variable stub to redirect execution to the polymorphic viral code, which has been inserted in the last section of the host file;[2][3] the stub decrypts and executes a secondary region, known as the loader; finally, the loader runs in a separate thread within the infected process to eventually load the Sality payload.[2]

Sality may execute a malicious payload that deletes files with certain extensions and/or beginning with specific strings, terminates security-related processes and services, searches a user's address book for e-mail addresses to send spam messages,[4] and contacts a remote host. Sality may also download additional executable files to install other malware, and for the purpose of propagating pay per install applications. Sality may contain Trojan components; some variants may have the ability to steal sensitive personal or financial data (i.e. information stealers),[5] generate and relay spam, relay traffic via HTTP proxies, infect web sites, achieve distributed computing tasks such as password cracking, as well as other capabilities.[2]

Sality's downloader mechanism downloads and executes additional malware as listed in the URLs received using the peer-to-peer component. The distributed malware may share the same "code signature" as the Sality payload, which may provide attribution to one group and/or that they share a large portion of the code. The additional malware typically communicates with and reports to central command and control (C&C) servers located throughout the world. According to Symantec, the "combination of file infection mechanism and the fully decentralized peer-to-peer network [...] make Sality one of the most effective and resilient malware in today's threat landscape."[2]

Two versions of the botnet are currently active, versions 3 and 4. The malware circulated on those botnets are digitally signed by the attackers to prevent hostile takeover. In recent years, Sality has also included the use of rootkit techniques to maintain persistence on compromised systems and evade host-based detections, such as anti-virus software.[6]

32.2.2 Installation

Sality infects files in the affected computer. Most variants use a DLL that is dropped once in each computer. The DLL file is written to disk in two forms, for example:

- %SYSTEM%\wmdrtc32.dll

- %SYSTEM%\wmdrtc32.dl_

The DLL file contains the bulk of the virus code. The file with the extension ".dl_" is the compressed copy. Recent variants of Sality, such as Virus:Win32-Sality.AM, do not drop the DLL, but instead load it entirely in memory without writing it to disk. This variant, along with others, also drops a driver with a random file name in the folder %SYSTEM%\drivers. Other malware may also drop Sality in the computer. For example, a Sality variant detected as Virus:Win32-Sality.AU is dropped by Worm: Win32-Sality.AU.[1] Some variants of Sality, may also include a rootkit by creating a device with the name Device\amsint32 or \DosDevices\amsint32.[6]

32.2.3 Method of Propagation

File infection

Sality usually targets all files in drive C: that have .SCR or .EXE file extensions, beginning with the root folder. Infected files increase in size by a varying amount.

The virus also targets applications that run at each Windows start and frequently used applications, referenced by the following registry keys:

- HKCU\Software\Microsoft\Windows\ShellNoRoam\MUICache

- HKCU\Software\Microsoft\Windows\CurrentVersion\Run

- HKLM\Software\Microsoft\Windows\CurrentVersion\Run[1]

Sality avoids infecting particular files, in order to remain hidden in the computer:

- Files protected by System File Checker (SFC)

- Files under the %SystemRoot% folder

- Executables of several antivirus/firewall products by ignoring files that contain certain substrings

Removable drives and network shares

Some variants of Sality can infect legitimate files, which are then moved to available removable drives and network shares by enumerating all network share folders and resources of the local computer and all files in drive C: (beginning with the root folder). It infects the files it finds by adding a new code section to the host and inserting its malicious code into the newly added section. If a legitimate file exists, the malware will copy the file to the Temporary Files folder and then infect the file. The resulting infected file is then moved to the root of all available removable drives and network shares as any of the following:

- \<random file name>.pif

- \<random file name>.exe

- \<random file name>.cmd

The Sality variant also creates an "autorun.inf" file in the root of all these drives that points to the virus copy. When a drive is accessed from a computer supporting the AutoRun feature, the virus is then launched automatically.[1] Some Sality variants may also drop a file with a .tmp file extension to the discovered network shares and resources as well as drop a .LNK file to run the dropped virus.[7]

32.2.4 Payload

- Sality may inject code into running processes by installing a message hook[8]

- Sality commonly searches for and attempts to delete files related to antivirus updates and terminate security applications, such as antivirus and personal firewall programs; attempts to terminate security applications containing the same strings as the files it avoids infecting; and may also terminate security-related services and block access to security-related websites that contain certain substrings[1][2][3][7][9][10][11][12][13][14][15][16]

- Sality variants may modify the computer registry to lower Windows security, disable the use of the Windows Registry Editor and/or prevent the viewing of files with hidden attributes; Some Sality variants recursively delete all registry values and data under the registry subkeys for HKCU\System\CurrentControlSet\Control\SafeBoot and HKLM\System\CurrentControlSet\Control\SafeBoot to prevent the user from starting Windows in safe mode[1][4][7][9][10][17][18][19]

- Some Sality variants can steal sensitive information such as cached passwords and logged keystrokes, which were entered on the affected computer[1][12][14]

- Sality variants usually attempt to download and execute other files including pay per install executables using a preconfigured list of up to 1000 peers; the goal of the P2P network is to exchange lists of URLs to feed to the downloader functionality; the files are downloaded into the Windows Temporary Files folder and decrypted using one of several hardcoded passwords[1][2][3][5][8][9][10][11][12][13][14][15][17][19][20]

- Most of Sality's payload is executed in the context of other processes, which makes cleaning difficult and allows the malware to bypass some firewalls; to avoid multiple injections in the same process, a system-wide mutex called "<process name>.exeM_<process ID>_" is created for every process in which code is injected, which would prevent more than one instance from running in memory at the same time.[1]

- Some variants of Win32-Sality drop a driver with a random file name in the folder %SYSTEM%\drivers to perform similar functions such as terminate security-related processes and block access to security-related websites, and may also disable any system service descriptor table (SSDT) hooks to prevent certain security software from working properly[1][2][3][9][10][11][17][19][21][22]

- Some Sality variants spread by moving to available removable/remote drives and network shares[1][2][3][7][8][10][11][19]

- Some Sality variants drop .LNK files, which automatically run the dropped virus[7]

- Some Sality variants may search a user's Outlook address book and Internet Explorer cached files for e-mail addresses to send spam messages, which then sends out spammed messages based on information it retrieves from a remote server[4]

- Sality may add a section to the configuration file %SystemRoot%\system.ini as an infection marker, contact remote hosts to confirm Internet connectivity, report a new infection to its author, receive configuration or other data, download and execute arbitrary files (including updates or additional malware), receive instruction from a remote attacker, and/or upload data taken from the affected computer; some Sality Variants may open a remote connection, allowing a remote attacker to download and execute arbitrary files on the infected computer[4][8][10][11][12][13][14][15][17][19][20]

- Computers infected with recent versions of Sality, such as Virus:Win32-Sality.AT, and Virus: Win32-Sality.AU, connect to other infected computers by joining a peer-to-peer (P2P) network to receive URLs pointing to additional malware components; the P2P protocol runs over UDP, all the messages exchanged on the P2P network are encrypted, and the local UDP port number used to connect to the network is generated as a function of the computer name[1]

- Sality may add a rootkit that includes a driver with capabilities such as terminating processes via NtTerminateProcess as well as blocking access to select anti-virus resources (e.g. anti-virus vendor web sites) by way of IP Filtering; the latter requires the driver to register a callback function, which will be used to determine if packets should be dropped or forwarded (e.g. drop packets if string contains the name of an anti-virus vendor from a comprised list)[6]

32.3 Recovery

Microsoft has identified dozens of files which are all commonly associated with the malware. [1] [4] [7] [8] [9] [10] [11] [12] [13] [14] [15] [16] [20] [21] [22] [23] [24][25][26] Sality uses stealth measures to maintain persistence on a system; thus, users may need to boot to a trusted environment in order to remove it. Sality may also make configuration changes such as to the Windows Registry, which makes it difficult to download, install and/or update virus protection. Also, since many variants of Sality attempt to propagate to available removable/remote drives and network shares, it is important to ensure the recovery process thoroughly detects and removes the malware from any and all known/possible locations.

32.4 See also

- Computer virus

- Botnet

32.5 References

[1] Microsoft Malware Protection Center (2010-08-07). "Win32-Sality". Microsoft. Archived from the original on 2013-09-17. Retrieved 2012-04-22.

[2] Nicolas Falliere (2011-08-03). "Sality: Story of a Peer-to-Peer Viral Network" (PDF). Symantec. Retrieved 2012-01-12.

[3] Angela Thigpen and Eric Chien (2010-05-20). "W32.Sality". Symantec. Archived from the original on 2013-10-05. Retrieved 2012-04-22.

[4] Microsoft Malware Protection Center (2009-05-29). "Win32-Sality.A". Microsoft. Retrieved 2012-04-22.

[5] FireEye, Inc (2012-02-14). "FireEye Advanced Threat Report - 2H 2011" (PDF). FireEye. Archived from the original (PDF) on 2012-05-22. Retrieved 2012-04-22.

[6] Artem I. Baranov (2013-01-15). "Sality Rootkit Analysis". Archived from the original on 2013-08-10. Retrieved 2013-01-19.

[7] Microsoft Malware Protection Center (2010-07-30). "Worm:Win32-Sality.AU". Microsoft. Archived from the original on 2013-09-27. Retrieved 2012-04-22. External link in |title= (help)

[8] Microsoft Malware Protection Center (2010-04-28). "Virus:Win32-Sality.G.dll". Microsoft. Retrieved 2012-04-22.

[9] Microsoft Malware Protection Center (2010-06-28). "Virus:Win32-Sality.AH". Microsoft. Retrieved 2012-04-22. External link in |title= (help)

[10] Microsoft Malware Protection Center (2010-08-27). "Virus:Win32-Sality.gen!AT". Microsoft. Retrieved 2012-04-22.

[11] Microsoft Malware Protection Center (2010-10-21). "Virus:Win32-Sality.gen!Q". Microsoft. Retrieved 2012-04-22.

[12] Microsoft Malware Protection Center (2008-07-03). "Virus:Win32-Sality.R". Microsoft. Archived from the original on 2014-04-04. Retrieved 2012-04-22.

[13] Microsoft Malware Protection Center (2008-07-07). "Virus:Win32-Sality.T". Microsoft. Archived from the original on 2014-04-04. Retrieved 2012-04-22.

[14] Microsoft Malware Protection Center (2008-07-07). "Virus:Win32-Sality.AN". Microsoft. Retrieved 2012-04-22. External link in |title= (help)

[15] Microsoft Malware Protection Center (2009-03-06). "Virus:Win32-Sality.S". Microsoft. Retrieved 2012-04-22.

[16] Microsoft Malware Protection Center (2008-07-08). "Virus:Win32-Sality". Microsoft. Archived from the original on 2012-01-01. Retrieved 2012-04-22.

[17] Microsoft Malware Protection Center (2010-07-30). "Virus:Win32-Sality.AU". Microsoft. Archived from the original on 2013-09-27. Retrieved 2012-04-22. External link in |title= (help)

[18] Microsoft Malware Protection Center (2010-07-30). "TrojanDropper:Win32-Sality.AU". Microsoft. Retrieved 2012-04-22. External link in |title= (help)

[19] Microsoft Malware Protection Center (2010-04-26). "Virus:Win32-Sality.AT". Microsoft. Archived from the original on 2014-01-30. Retrieved 2012-04-22. External link in |title= (help)

[20] Microsoft Malware Protection Center (2007-11-16). "Virus:Win32-Sality.M". Microsoft. Archived from the original on 2014-04-05. Retrieved 2012-04-22.

[21] Microsoft Malware Protection Center (2010-08-10). "Trojan:WinNT-Sality". Microsoft. Archived from the original on 2013-12-05. Retrieved 2012-04-22.

[22] Microsoft Malware Protection Center (2010-09-17). "WinNT-Sality". Microsoft. Retrieved 2012-04-22.

[23] Microsoft Malware Protection Center (2010-04-14). "Virus:Win32-Sality.G". Microsoft. Archived from the original on 2014-04-05. Retrieved 2012-04-22.

[24] Microsoft Malware Protection Center (2008-07-08). "Virus:Win32-Sality.AM". Microsoft. Archived from the original on 2013-12-09. Retrieved 2012-04-22. External link in |title= (help)

[25] Microsoft Malware Protection Center (2009-06-17). "Virus:Win32-Sality.gen!P". Microsoft. Retrieved 2012-04-22.

[26] Microsoft Malware Protection Center (2009-09-02). "Virus:Win32-Sality.gen". Microsoft. Retrieved 2012-04-22. External link in |title= (help)

Chapter 33

Slenfbot

Slenfbot is the classification for a family of malicious software (malware), which infects files on Microsoft Windows systems. Slenfbot was first discovered in 2007 and, since then, numerous variants have followed; each with slightly different characteristics and new additions to the worm's payload, such as the ability to provide the attacker with unauthorized access to the compromised host. Slenfbot primarily spreads by luring users to follow links to websites, which contain a malicious payload. Slenfbot propagates via instant messaging applications, removable drives and/or the local network via network shares. The code for Slenfbot appears to be closely managed, which may provide attribution to a single group and/or indicate that a large portion of the code is shared amongst multiple groups. The inclusion of other malware families and variants as well as its own continuous evolution, makes Slenfbot a highly effective downloader with a propensity to cause even more damage to compromised systems.

33.1 Aliases

The majority of Antivirus (A/V) vendors use the following naming conventions when referring to this family of malware (the * at the end of the names is a wildcard for all the possible classifications and/or distinctions for this malware family):

- Slenfbot

- Stekct

33.2 Publicly Known Efforts

None publicly known.

33.3 Malware Profile

33.3.1 Summary

Slenfbot is a worm that spreads using links to websites containing malicious software (malware) via instant messaging programs, which may include MSN/Windows Live Messenger, AOL Instant Messenger (AIM), Yahoo Messenger, Google Chat, Facebook Chat, ICQ and Skype. The worm propagates automatically via removable drives and shares, or on the local network through the Windows file sharing service (i.e., Server or LanmanServer service). Slenfbot also contains backdoor capabilities that allow unauthorized access to an affected machine.[1][2][3][4][5][6] The code appears to be closely controlled, which may provide attribution to one group and/or that the malware authors share a significant portion of the code. Slenfbot has been seen in the wild since 2007, obtained new features and capabilities over time, and subsequent variants have systematically gained similar, if not the same, feature sets. Because of this, Slenfbot continues to operate as an effective infector and dynamic downloader of additional malware; thus, making it a highly functional delivery mechanism for other spyware, information stealers, spam bots as well as other malware.[4]

33.3.2 Installation

When executed, Slenfbot copies a duplicate of the malicious payload to the %SYSTEM% folder with a filename, which varies per the particular variant and sets the attributes for the copy to read only, hidden and system to hide the contents in Windows Explorer. The worm then makes changes to the registry to maintain persistence so that the malware executes a duplicate copy on each subsequent startup of the system (e.g. copying the malicious executable to the HKLM\Software\Microsoft\Windows\CurrentVersion\Run subkey). Several variants may modify the registry during installation to add the malware to the list of applications that are authorized to access the Internet; thus, allowing the malware to communicate without raising Windows security alerts and run unimpeded by the Windows Firewall.[1][2][3][4][5][6]

In some cases, variants may instead modify the registry to install the malicious payload as a debugger for the benign system file ctfmon.exe so that ctfmon.exe executes on system startup, which leads to the execution of the malware.[1]

In most cases, Slenfbot will attempt to delete the original copy of the worm. Some variants may make additional modifications to the registry in order to delete the originally executed copy of the worm when the system restarts.[1][2][3][5][6]

Some Slenfbot variants may, on initial execution, test to see if MSN/Windows Live Messenger is currently running by looking for a window with the class name "MSBLWindow-Class". If the worm finds the window, the malware may display a fake error message.[1]

If Slenfbot is launched from a removable drive, some variants may open Windows Explorer and display the contents of the affected drive. Certain Slenfbot variants may inject a thread into explorer.exe, which periodically checks for the presence of the malware in the System folder. If the file is not found, the malware downloads a new copy from a specified server and launches the new copy.[1][4][6]

33.3.3 Method of Propagation

Instant Messaging

Slenfbot uses instant messaging as an attack vector to spread the worm to other accounts and contacts. The remote attacker may use the worm's backdoor capabilities to instruct Slenfbot to spread via MSN/Windows Live Messenger, AOL Instant Messenger (AIM), Yahoo Messenger, Google Chat, Facebook Chat, ICQ and Skype. The worm connects to a remote server and sends a copy of a URL, which contains a list of possible messages to send randomly; creates a ZIP archive, which contains a copy of the malware; and then sends the ZIP archive to other instant messaging client contacts.[1][2][3][4][5][6] Following are some examples of the messages the worm may spread:

- Are you serious...is this really you?

- HAHA! this is funnny! here, read this guys shirt.

- Is this really a pic of you?

- OMFG look at this!!!

- This is my dream car right here! [5]

The ZIP file includes a file name for the Slenfbot executable, and may also contain a URL for a file to download in situations where the attacker instructs the worm to send arbitrary file(s).[1][5][6]

Removable Drives

Slenfbot may spread to removable drives by creating a directory called "RECYCLER" in the root directory of the removable drive. The malware will then create a subdirectory in the "RECYCLER" folder (e.g. "S-1-6-21-1257894210-1075856346-012573477-2315"), and copy the malicious payload to the directory using a different name for the executable (e.g. "folderopen.exe"). Slenfbot may also create an autorun.inf file in the root directory of the drive so that the worm may execute if the drive is connected to another system.[1][6]

Certain variants may download an updated copy of Slenfbot from a location specified in the worm, and write the file to a directory (e.g. using the name "~secure"). For all the locations the worm copies itself to, Slenfbot sets the hidden and system attributes on the respective directories and files.[1][5][6] In some circumstances due to a programming issue, Slenfbot may only create one directory rather than two (e.g. "E:\RECYCLERS-1-6-21-1257894210-1075856346-012573477-2315\folderopen.exe").[1]

File and Print Shares

Slenfbot may spread to accessible shares upon successful compromise of a system. The worm may also spread to file and print shares by exploiting known vulnerabilities such as MS06-040 or MS10-061, which pertain to issues with the Server and Print Spooler services, respectively. The attacker would have to instruct the worm to spread to the remote system via exploit or instant messaging in order to continue the propagation of Slenfbot.[1][5][6][7][8]

33.3.4 Payload

- Slenfbot attempts to connect to an Internet Relay Chat (IRC) server via a particular TCP port (the IRC channel and port number may vary per the variant), joins a channel and then waits for commands; the attacker may then use the backdoor to perform additional actions on the compromised system such as delete the malware, join another IRC channel, download/execute arbitrary files and/or propagate to other instant messaging accounts [1][5][6]

- Slenfbot makes modifications to the hosts file by replacing %SYSTEM%\drivers\etc.\hosts with a file of its own; the modified host file may contain several entries to point various anti-virus and security related domains to localhost (i.e. 127.0.0.1) or to a random IP address, which obstruct the user from visiting the list of domains; the file may also contain numerous blank lines to give the appearance that the hosts file has not been modified [1][5]

- Slenfbot runs commands to delete files named *.zip and *.com in the current directory as well as the user's "Received Files" directory, which is the default location where Windows Messenger stores downloaded files; the latter may be to delete the original copy of the worm, which was received via Windows Messenger [1]

- Some Slenfbot variants may create a file (e.g. "RemoveMexxxx.bat") in the %TEMP% directory, which is a batch file that tries to delete the copy after execution to prevent detection [5]

- Slenfbot deletes various registry keys and any subkeys and values that they may contain in order to disable system restore, task manager, the use of the Windows Registry Editor and/or prevent the viewing of files with hidden attributes; the worm may also disable antivirus, firewall as well as attempt to disable Data Execution Prevention (DEP) by making other modifications to the system; some variants may periodically rewrite the changes in order to maintain persistence on the system [1][2][3][5][6]

- Slenfbot may terminate security-related processes as well as stop, disable and delete services on the compromised system in order to remain undetected and maintain persistence [1][6]

- Slenfbot may inject code into the Explorer process to "lock" the file in order to prevent the worm from being deleted and/or to reopen the payload upon process termination [4]

- Slenfbot may also be capable of hiding the malicious process from task manager [4][5]

- Slenfbot variants may create a mutex that differs according to variant [1]

- Slenfbot may execute additional commands after receiving data from another remote system; commands may include additional instructions to further modify the compromised system [1][6]

- Slenfbot may download and install additional malware to relay spam, steal information, install spyware toolbars as well as propagate other malicious campaigns; the initial Slenfbot payload serves as a first-stage downloader for the purpose of loading additional malware on the compromised host [1][3][4][5][6]

33.4   Prevention

The following steps may help prevent infection:

- Get the latest computer updates for all your installed software

- Use up-to-date antivirus software

- Limit user privileges on the computer

- Have the sender confirm that they sent the link before clicking on it

- Use caution when clicking on links to webpages

- Use caution when opening attachments and accepting file transfers

- Use online services to analyze files and URLs (e.g. Malwr,[9] VirusTotal,[10] Anubis,[11] Wepawet,[12] etc.)

- Only run software from publishers you trust

- Protect yourself against social engineering attacks

- Use strong passwords and change passwords periodically [1][2][3][13][14]

33.5   Recovery

Slenfbot uses stealth measures to maintain persistence on a system; thus, you may need to boot to a trusted environment in order to remove it. Slenfbot may also make changes to your computer such as changes to the Windows Registry, which makes it difficult to download, install and/or update your virus protection. Also, since many variants of Slenfbot attempt to propagate to available removable/remote drives and network shares, it is important to ensure the recovery process thoroughly detects and removes the malware from any and all known/possible locations.

One possible solution would be to use Microsoft's Windows Defender Offline Beta to detect and remove Slenfbot from your system. For more information on Windows Defender Offline, go to: http://windows.microsoft.com/en-US/windows/what-is-windows-defender-offline [1][2][3]

33.6   See also

- Computer virus

- Botnet

33.7 References

[1] Microsoft Malware Protection Center (2008-08-26). "Win32/Slenfbot". Microsoft. Retrieved 2012-06-17.

[2] Microsoft Malware Protection Center (2012-02-15). "Worm:Win32/Stekct.A". Microsoft. Retrieved 2012-06-17.

[3] Microsoft Malware Protection Center (2012-02-29). "Worm:Win32/Stekct.B". Microsoft. Retrieved 2012-06-17.

[4] Microsoft Malware Protection Center (2008-09-17). "Win32/Slenfbot - Just Another IRC bot?". Hamish O'Dea. Retrieved 2012-06-17.

[5] Methusela Cebrian Ferrer (2008-10-01). "Win32/Slenfbot". CA Technologies. Retrieved 2012-06-17.

[6] ESET Threat Encyclopaedia (2011-01-17). "Win32/Slenfbot.AD". ESET. Retrieved 2012-06-17.

[7] Microsoft Security Tech Center (2006-08-08). "Microsoft Security Bulletin MS06-040". Microsoft. Retrieved 2012-06-17.

[8] Microsoft Security Tech Center (2010-09-14). "Microsoft Security Bulletin MS10-061". Microsoft. Retrieved 2012-06-17.

[9] "Malwr.com". Retrieved 2012-06-17.

[10] "VirusTotal". Retrieved 2012-06-17.

[11] "Anubis". Retrieved 2012-06-17.

[12] "Wepawet". Retrieved 2012-06-17.

[13] Kurt Avish (2012-05-22). "Stekct.Evl". Sparking Dawn. Retrieved 2012-06-17.

[14] Maninder Singh (2012-05-22). "Stekct.Evi". HackTik. Retrieved 2012-06-17.

Chapter 34

Srizbi botnet

Srizbi BotNet, also known by its aliases of **Nug's BotNet** and **GameFreakChan**, was considered one of the world's largest botnet, and has been responsible for sending out more than half of all the spam being sent by all the major botnets combined.[1][2]<ref ="SecurityWeek">Kovacs, Eduard (August 28, 2014). "Cybercriminals Attempt to Revive Srizbi Spam Botnet". SecurityWeek. Retrieved 2016-01-05.</ref> The botnets consist of computers infected by the Srizbi trojan, which sends spam on command. The botnet suffered a significant setback in November 2008 when hosting provider Janka Cartel was taken down; global spam volumes reduced by up to 93% as a result of this action.

34.1 Size

The size of the Srizbi botnet is estimated to be around 450,000[3] compromised machines, with estimation differences being smaller than 5% among various sources.[2][4] The botnet is reported to be capable of sending around 60 Trillion Janka Threats a day, which is more than half of the total of the approximately 100 trillion Janka Threats sent every day. As a comparison, the highly publicized Storm botnet only manages to reach around 20% of the total amount of spam sent during its peak periods.[2][5]

The Srizbi botnet is showing a relative decline after an aggressive growth in the amount of spam messages sent out in mid-2008. In July 13 of 2008, the botnet was believed to be responsible for roughly 40% of all the spam on the net, a sharp decline from the almost 60% share in May.[6]

34.2 Origins

The earliest reports on Srizbi trojan outbreaks were around June 2007, with small differences in detection dates across antivirus software vendors.[7][8] However, reports indicate that the first released version had already been assembled on 31 March 2007.[9] The Srizbi botnet by some experts is considered the second largest botnet of the Internet.

However, there is controversy surrounding the Kraken botnet.[10][11][12][13] As of 2008, it may be that Srizbi is the largest botnet.

34.3 Spread and botnet composition

The Srizbi botnet consists of computers which have been infected by the Srizbi trojan horse. This trojan horse is deployed onto its victim computer through the Mpack malware kit.[14] Past editions have used the "n404 web exploit kit" malware kit to spread, but this kit's usage has been deprecated in favor of Mpack.[15]

The distribution of these malware kits is partially achieved by utilizing the botnet itself. The botnet has been known to send out spam containing links to fake videos about celebrities, which include a link pointing to the malware kit. Similar attempts have been taken with other subjects such as illegal software sales and personal messages.[16][17][18] Apart from this self-propagation, the MPack kit is also known for much more aggressive spreading tactics, most notably the compromise of about 10,000 websites in June 2007.[19] These domains, which included a surprising number of pornographic websites,[20] ended up forwarding the unsuspecting visitor to websites containing the MPack program.

Once a computer becomes infected by the trojan horse, the computer becomes known as a zombie, which will then be at the command of the controller of the botnet, commonly referred to as the botnet herder.[21] The operation of the Srizbi botnet is based upon a number of servers which control the utilization of the individual bots in the botnet. These servers are redundant copies of each other, which protects the botnet from being crippled in case a system failure or legal action takes a server down. These servers are generally placed in countries such as Russia, where law enforcement against digital crime is limited.

34.3.1 Reactor Mailer

The server-side of the Srizbi botnet is handled by a program called "Reactor Mailer", which is a Python-based web component responsible for coordinating the spam sent out by the individual bots in the botnet. Reactor Mailer has existed since 2004, and is currently in its third release, which is also used to control the Srizbi botnet. The software allows for secure login and allows multiple accounts, which strongly suggests that access to the botnet and its spam capacity is sold to external parties (Software as a service). This is further reinforced by evidence showing that the Srizbi botnet runs multiple batches of spam at a time; blocks of IP addresses can be observed sending different types of spam at any one time. Once a user has been granted access, he or she can utilize the software to create the message they want to send, test it for its SpamAssassin score and after that send it to all the users in a list of email addresses.

Suspicion has arisen that the writer of the Reactor Mailer program might be the same person responsible for the Srizbi trojan, as code analysis shows a code fingerprint that matches between the two programs. If this claim is indeed true, then this coder might well be responsible for the trojan behind another botnet, named Rustock. According to Symantec, the code used in the Srizbi trojan is very similar to the code found in the Rustock trojan, and could well be an improved version of the latter.[22]

34.3.2 Srizbi trojan

The Srizbi trojan is the client side program responsible for sending the spam from infected machines. The trojan has been credited with being extremely efficient at this task, which explains why Srizbi is capable of sending such high volumes of spam without having a huge numerical advantage in the number of infected computers.

Apart from having an efficient spam engine, the trojan is also very capable in hiding itself from both the user and the system itself, including any products designed to remove the trojan from the system. The trojan itself is fully executed in kernel mode and has been noted to employ rootkit technologies to prevent any form of detection.[23] By patching the NTFS file system drivers, the trojan will make its files invisible for both the operating system and any human user utilizing the system. The trojan is also capable of hiding network traffic it generates by directly attaching NDIS and TCP/IP drivers to its own process, a feature currently unique for this trojan. This procedure has been proven to allow the trojan to bypass both firewall and sniffer protection provided locally on the system.[22]

Once the bot is in place and operational, it will contact one of the hardcoded servers from a list it carries with it. This server will then supply the bot with a zip file containing a number of files required by the bot to start its spamming business. The following files have been identified to be downloaded:

1. 000_data2 - mail server domains

2. 001_ncommall - list of names

3. 002_senderna - list of possible sender names

4. 003_sendersu - list of possible sender surnames

5. config - Main spam configuration file

6. message - HTML message to spam

7. mlist - Recipients mail addresses

8. mxdata - MX record data

When these files have been received, the bot will first initialize a software routine which allows it to remove files critical for revealing spam and rootkit applications. [22] After this procedure is done, the trojan will then start sending out the spam message it has received from the control server.

34.4 Incidents

The Srizbi botnet has been the basis for several incidents which have received media coverage. Several of the most notable ones will be described below here. This is by no means a complete list of incidents, but just a list of the major ones.

34.4.1 The "Ron Paul" incident

In October 2007, several anti-spam firms noticed an unusual political spam campaign emerging. Unlike the usual messages about counterfeit watches, stocks, or penis enlargement, the mail contained promotional information about United States presidential candidate Ron Paul. The Ron Paul camp dismissed the spam as being not related to the official presidential campaign. A spokesman told the press: "If it is true, it could be done by a well-intentioned yet misguided supporter or someone with bad intentions trying to embarrass the campaign. Either way, this is independent work, and we have no connection."[24]

The spam was ultimately confirmed as having come from the Srizbi network.[25] Through the capture of one of the control servers involved,[26] investigators learned that the spam message had been sent to up to 160 million email addresses by as few as 3,000 bot computers. The spammer has only been identified by his Internet handle "nenastnyj" (*Ненастный*, means "rainy" or "foul", as in "rainy day, foul weather" in Russian); his or her real identity has not been determined.

34.4.2 Malicious spam tripling volumes in a week

In the week from 20 June 2008 Srizbi managed to triple the amount of malicious spam sent from an average 3% to 9.9%, largely due to its own effort.[27] This particular spam wave was an aggressive attempt to increase the size of the Srizbi botnet by sending emails to users which warned them that they had been videotaped naked.[28] Sending this message, which is a kind of spam referred to as "Stupid Theme", was an attempt to get people to click the malicious link included in the mail, before realizing that this message was most likely spam. While old, this social engineering technique remains a proven method of infection for spammers.

The size of this operation shows that the power and monetary income from a botnet is closely based upon its spam capacity: more infected computers translate directly into greater revenue for the botnet controller. It also shows the power botnets have to increase their own size, mainly by using a part of their own strength in numbers.[29]

34.4.3 Server relocation

After the removal of the control servers hosted by McColo in late November 2008, the control of the botnet was transferred to servers hosted in Estonia. This was accomplished through a mechanism in the trojan horse that queried an algorithmically generated set of domain names, one of which was registered by the individuals controlling the botnet. The United States computer security firm FireEye, Inc. kept the system out of the controllers' hands for a period of two weeks by preemptively registering the generated domain names but was not in a position to sustain this effort. However the spamming activity was greatly reduced after this control server transfer.[30]

34.5   See also

- Botnet
- Storm botnet
- MPack malware kit
- Email spam
- Internet crime

- Internet security
- Operation: Bot Roast
- Shadowserver
- Helpful worm
- McColo
- Command and control (malware)
- Zombie (computer science)
- Alureon
- Conficker
- Gameover ZeuS
- Storm botnet
- Bagle (computer worm)
- ZeroAccess botnet
- Regin (malware)
- Zeus (malware)

34.6   References

[1] Jackson Higgins, Kelly (May 8, 2008). "Srizbi Botnet Sending Over 60 Billion Spams a Day". Dark Reading. Retrieved 2008-07-20.

[2] Pauli, Darren (May 8, 2008). "Srizbi Botnet Sets New Records for Spam". PC World. Retrieved 2008-07-20.

[3] "Spam on rise after brief reprieve". *BBC News*. 2008-11-26. Retrieved 2010-05-23.

[4] Popa, Bogdan (April 10, 2008). "Meet Srizbi, the Largest Botnet Ever". Softpedia. Retrieved 2008-07-20.

[5] E. Dunn, John (May 13, 2008). "Srizbi Grows Into World's Largest Botnet". CSO Online. Retrieved 2008-07-20.

[6] "Spam statistics from TRACE". Marshall. July 13, 2008. Retrieved 2008-07-20. |first1= missing |last1= in Authors list (help)

[7] "Trojan.Srizbi". Symantec. July 23, 2007. Retrieved 2008-07-20.

[8] "Troj/RKAgen-A Trojan (Rootkit.Win32.Agent.ea, Trojan.Srizbi) - Sophos security analysis". Sophos. August 2007. Retrieved 2008-07-20.

[9] Stewart, Joe. "Inside the "Ron Paul" Spam Botnet". *Secureworks.com*. SecureWorks. Retrieved 9 March 2016.

[10] Higgins, Kelly Jackson (2008-04-07). "New Massive Botnet Twice the Size of Storm". *darkreading.com*. London, UK: UBM plc. Retrieved 2014-01-09.

[11] Higgins, Kelly Jackson (2008-05-08). "Srizbi Botnet Sending Over 60 Billion Spams a Day". *darkreading.com*. London, UK: UBM plc. Retrieved 2014-01-09.

[12] "Internet reputation system". TrustedSource. 2013-09-17. Retrieved 2014-01-09.

[13] "Kraken, Not New But Still Newsworthy? - F-Secure Weblog : News from the Lab". F-secure.com. 2008-04-09. Retrieved 2014-01-09.

[14] Keizer, Gregg (July 5, 2007). "Mpack installs ultra-invisible Trojan". ComputerWorld. Retrieved 2008-07-20.

[15] Stewart, Joe. "Inside the "Ron Paul" Spam Botnet". *Secureworks.com*. SecureWorks. Retrieved 9 March 2016.

[16] Blog, TRACE (March 7, 2008). "Srizbi uses multi-pronged attack to spread malware". Marshal Limited. Retrieved 2008-07-20.

[17] McKenzie, Grey (June 25, 2008). "Srizbi Botnet Is Largely Responsible for Recent Sharp Increase In Spam". National Cyber Security. Archived from the original on August 28, 2008. Retrieved 2008-07-20.

[18] "Srizbi spam uses celebrities as lures". TRACE Blog. February 20, 2008. Retrieved 2008-07-20.

[19] Keizer, Gregg (June 10, 2007). "Hackers compromise 10k sites, launch 'phenomenal' attack". ComputerWorld. Retrieved 2008-07-20.

[20] Keizer, Gregg (June 22, 2007). "Porn sites serve up Mpack attacks". ComputerWorld. Retrieved 2008-07-20.

[21] "Spying on bot nets becoming harder". SecurityFocus. October 12, 2006. Retrieved 2008-07-20.

[22] Hayashi, Kaoru (June 29, 2007). "Spam from the Kernel: Full-Kernel Malware Installed by MPack". Symantec. Retrieved 2008-07-20.

[23] Dan Goodin (2009-02-11). "Microsoft takes scissors to Srizbi". San Francisco: The Register. Retrieved 2009-02-10.

[24] Cheng, Jacqui (October 31, 2007). "Researchers: Ron Paul campaign e-mails originating from spambots". ARS Technica. Retrieved 2008-07-20.

[25] Paul, Ryan (December 6, 2007). "Researchers track Ron Paul spam back to Reactor botnet". ARS Technica. Retrieved 2008-07-20.

[26] Stewart, Joe. "Inside the "Ron Paul" Spam Botnet". *Secureworks.com*. Secureworks. Retrieved 9 March 2016.

[27] Salek, Negar (June 25, 2008). "One of the biggest threats to Internet users today: Srizbi". SC Magazine. Retrieved 2008-07-20.

[28] "The Naked Truth About the Srizbi Botnet". Protect Web Form Blog. May 19, 2008. Retrieved 2008-07-20.

[29] Walsh, Sue (June 27, 2008). "Spam Volume Triples In A Week". All Spammed Up. Retrieved 2008-07-20.

[30] Keizer, Gregg (November 26, 2008). "Massive botnet returns from the dead, starts spamming". Computerworld. Retrieved 2009-01-24.

Chapter 35

Stacheldraht

Stacheldraht (German for barbed wire) is a piece of software written by Random for Linux and Solaris systems which acts as a distributed denial of service (DDoS) agent. This tool detects and automatically enables source address forgery.

Stacheldraht uses a number of different DoS attacks, including UDP flood, ICMP flood, TCP SYN flood and Smurf attack.

It combines features of Trinoo with TFN, and adds encryption.

35.1 See also

- Low Orbit Ion Cannon A stress test tool that has been used for DDoS attacks

- High Orbit Ion Cannon The replacement for LOIC used in DDoS attacks

- Fork bomb

- Denial-of-service attack

- Slowloris (computer security)

- ReDoS

35.2 External links

- Dittrich summary of Stacheldraht features

- Dittrich analysis of Stacheldraht

- Stacheldraht v4 source code

Chapter 36

Storm botnet

Not to be confused with the unrelated Eggdrop bot script "stormbot.tcl.".
For more details on the worm, see Storm Worm.

The **Storm botnet** or **Storm worm botnet** (also known

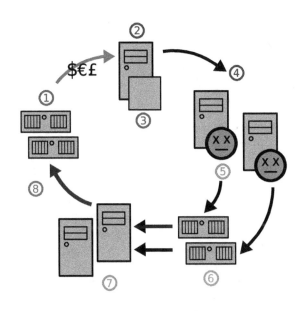

The typical lifecycle of spam that originates from a botnet: (1) Spammer's web site (2) Spammer (3) Spamware (4) Infected computers (5) Virus or trojan (6) Mail servers (7) Users (8) Web traffic

as **Dorf botnet** and **Ecard malware**[1]) is a remotely controlled network of "zombie" computers (or "botnet") that have been linked by the Storm Worm, a Trojan horse spread through e-mail spam. At its height in September 2007, the Storm botnet was running on anywhere from 1 million to 50 million computer systems,[2][3] and accounted for 8% of all malware on Microsoft Windows computers.[4] It was first identified around January 2007, having been distributed by email with subjects such as "230 dead as storm batters Europe," giving it its well-known name. The botnet began to decline in late 2007, and by mid-2008, had been reduced to infecting about 85,000 computers, far less than it had in-

fected a year earlier.[5]

As of December 2012, the original creators of Storm still haven't been found. The Storm botnet has displayed defensive behaviors that indicated that its controllers were actively protecting the botnet against attempts at tracking and disabling it, by specifically attacking the online operations of some security vendors and researchers who had attempted to investigate it.[6] Security expert Joe Stewart revealed that in late 2007, the operators of the botnet began to further decentralize their operations, in possible plans to sell portions of the Storm botnet to other operators. It was reportedly powerful enough to force entire countries off the Internet, and was estimated to be capable of executing more instructions per second than some of the world's top supercomputers.[7] The United States Federal Bureau of Investigation considered the botnet a major risk to increased bank fraud, identity theft, and other cybercrimes.[8][9]

36.1 Origins

First detected on the Internet in January 2007, the Storm botnet and worm are so-called because of the storm-related subject lines its infectious e-mail employed initially, such as "230 dead as storm batters Europe." Later provocative subjects included, "Chinese missile shot down USA aircraft," and "U.S. Secretary of State Condoleezza Rice has kicked German Chancellor Angela Merkel."[2][10][11] It is suspected by some information security professionals that well-known fugitive spammers, including Leo Kuvayev, may have been involved in the operation and control of the Storm botnet.[12] According to technology journalist Daniel Tynan, writing under his "Robert X. Cringely" pseudonym, a great portion of the fault for the existence of the Storm botnet lay with Microsoft and Adobe Systems.[13] Other sources state that Storm Worm's primary method of victim acquisition was through enticing users via frequently changing social engineering (confidence trickery) schemes.[14] According to Patrick Runald, the Storm botnet had a strong American focus, and likely had agents working to support it within the United States.[15] Some experts, however, believe the Storm botnet controllers were Russian, some pointing specifically at the Russian Business Network, citing that the Storm software mentions a hatred of the Moscow-based security firm Kaspersky Lab, and includes the Russian word *"buldozhka,"* which means "bulldog."[16]

36.2 Composition

The botnet, or zombie network, comprises computers running Microsoft Windows as their operating system.[17] Once infected, a computer becomes known as a bot. This bot then performs automated tasks—anything from gathering data on the user, to attacking web sites, to forwarding infected e-mail—without its owner's knowledge or permission. Estimates indicate that 5,000 to 6,000 computers are dedicated to propagating the spread of the worm through the use of e-mails with infected attachments; 1.2 billion virus messages have been sent by the botnet through September 2007, including a record 57 million on August 22, 2007 alone.[17] Lawrence Baldwin, a computer forensics specialist, was quoted as saying, "Cumulatively, Storm is sending billions of messages a day. It could be double digits in the billions, easily."[2] One of the methods used to entice victims to infection-hosting web sites are offers of free music, for artists such as Beyoncé Knowles, Kelly Clarkson, Rihanna, The Eagles, Foo Fighters, R. Kelly, and Velvet Revolver.[18] Signature-based detection, the main defense of most computer systems against virus and malware infections, is hampered by the large number of Storm variants.[19]

Back-end servers that control the spread of the botnet and Storm worm automatically re-encode their distributed infection software twice an hour, for new transmissions, making it difficult for anti-virus vendors to stop the virus and infection spread. Additionally, the location of the remote servers which control the botnet are hidden behind a constantly changing DNS technique called 'fast flux', making it difficult to find and stop virus hosting sites and mail servers. In short, the name and location of such machines are frequently changed and rotated, often on a minute by minute basis.[20] The Storm botnet's operators control the system via peer-to-peer techniques, making external monitoring and disabling of the system more difficult.[21][22] There is no central "command-and-control point" in the Storm botnet that can be shut down.[23] The botnet also makes use of encrypted traffic.[24] Efforts to infect computers usually revolve around convincing people to download e-mail attachments which contain the virus through subtle manipulation. In one instance, the botnet's controllers took advantage of the National Football League's opening weekend, sending out mail offering "football tracking programs"

which did nothing more than infect a user's computer.[25][26] According to Matt Sergeant, chief anti-spam technologist at MessageLabs, "In terms of power, [the botnet] utterly blows the supercomputers away. If you add up all 500 of the top supercomputers, it blows them all away with just 2 million of its machines. It's very frightening that criminals have access to that much computing power, but there's not much we can do about it."[17] It is estimated that only 10%−20% of the total capacity and power of the Storm botnet is currently being used.[27]

Computer security expert Joe Stewart detailed the process by which compromised machines join the botnet: attempts to join the botnet are made by launching a series of EXE files on the said machine, in stages. Usually, they are named in a sequence from *game0.exe* through *game5.exe*, or similar. It will then continue launching executables in turn. They typically perform the following:[28]

1. game0.exe - Backdoor/downloader

2. game1.exe - SMTP relay

3. game2.exe - E-mail address stealer

4. game3.exe - E-mail virus spreader

5. game4.exe - Distributed Denial of Service (DDoS) attack tool

6. game5.exe - Updated copy of Storm Worm dropper

At each stage the compromised system will connect into the botnet; fast flux DNS makes tracking this process exceptionally difficult. This code is run from *%windir%\system32\wincom32.sys* on a Windows system, via a kernel rootkit, and all connections back to the botnet are sent through a modified version of the eDonkey/Overnet communications protocol.

36.3 Methodology

The Storm botnet and its variants employ a variety of attack vectors, and a variety of defensive steps exist as well. The Storm botnet was observed to be defending itself, and attacking computer systems that scanned for Storm virus-infected computer systems online.[29] The botnet will defend itself with DDoS counter-attacks, to maintain its own internal integrity.[30] At certain points in time, the Storm worm used to spread the botnet has attempted to release hundreds or thousands of versions of itself onto the Internet, in a concentrated attempt to overwhelm the defenses of anti-virus and malware security firms.[31] According to Joshua Corman, an IBM security researcher, "This is the first time that I can remember ever seeing researchers who were actually afraid of investigating an exploit."[32] Researchers are still unsure if the botnet's defenses and counterattacks are a form of automation, or manually executed by the system's operators.[32] "If you try to attach a debugger, or query sites it's reporting into, it knows and punishes you instantaneously. [Over at] SecureWorks, a chunk of it DDoS-ed [distributed-denial-of-service attacked] a researcher off the network. Every time I hear of an investigator trying to investigate, they're automatically punished. It knows it's being investigated, and it punishes them. It fights back," Corman said.[1]

Spameater.com as well as other sites such as 419eater.com and Artists Against 419, both of which deal with 419 spam e-mail fraud, have experienced DDoS attacks, temporarily rendering them completely inoperable. The DDoS attacks consist of making massed parallel network calls to those and other target IP addresses, overloading the servers' capacities and preventing them from responding to requests.[33] Other anti-spam and anti-fraud groups, such as the Spamhaus Project, were also attacked. The webmaster of Artists Against 419 said that the website's server succumbed after the attack increased to over 100Mbit. Similar attacks were perpetrated against over a dozen anti-fraud site hosts. Jeff Chan, a spam researcher, stated, "In terms of mitigating Storm, it's challenging at best and impossible at worst since the bad guys control many hundreds of megabits of traffic. There's some evidence that they may control hundreds of Gigabits of traffic, which is enough to force some countries off the Internet."[7]

The Storm botnet's systems also take steps to defend itself locally, on victims' computer systems. The botnet, on some compromised systems, creates a computer process on the Windows machine that notifies the Storm systems whenever a new program or other processes begin. Previously, the Storm worms locally would tell the other programs — such as anti-virus, or anti-malware software, to simply not run. However, according to IBM security research, versions of Storm also now simply "fool" the local computer system to run the hostile program successfully, but in fact, they are not doing anything. "Programs, including not just AV exes, dlls and sys files, but also software such as the P2P applications BearShare and eDonkey, will appear to run successfully, even though they didn't actually do anything, which is far less suspicious than a process that gets terminated suddenly from the outside," said Richard Cohen of Sophos. Compromised users, and related security systems, will assume that security software is running successfully when it in fact is not.[34]

On September 17, 2007, a Republican Party website in the United States was compromised, and used to propagate the Storm worm and botnet.[35][36] In October 2007, the botnet took advantage of flaws in YouTube's captcha application on its mail systems, to send targeted spam e-mails to Xbox owners with a scam involving winning a special version of the video game *Halo 3*.[37] Other attack methods include using appealing animated images of laughing cats to get people to click on a trojan software download, and tricking users of Yahoo!'s GeoCities service to download software that was claimed to be needed to use GeoCities itself.[38][39] The GeoCities attack in particular was called a "full-fledged attack vector" by Paul Ferguson of Trend Micro, and implicated members of the Russian Business Network, a well-known spam and malware service.[39] On Christmas Eve in 2007, the Storm botnet began sending out holiday-themed messages revolving around male interest in women, with such titles as "Find Some Christmas Tail", "The Twelve Girls of Christmas," and "Mrs. Claus Is Out Tonight!" and photos of attractive women. It was described as an attempt to draw more unprotected systems into the botnet and boost its size over the holidays, when security updates from protection vendors may take longer to be distributed.[40][41] A day after the e-mails with Christmas strippers were distributed, the Storm botnet operators immediately began sending new infected e-mails that claimed to wish their recipients a "Happy New Year 2008!"[42]

In January 2008, the botnet was detected for the first time to be involved in phishing attacks against major financial institutions, targeting both Barclays and Halifax.[43]

36.4 Encryption and sales

Around October 15, 2007, it was uncovered that portions of the Storm botnet and its variants could be for sale.[44][45] This is being done by using unique security keys in the encryption of the botnet's Internet traffic and information.[24] The unique keys will allow each segment, or sub-section of the Storm botnet, to communicate with a section that has a matching security key. However, this may also allow people to detect, track, and block Storm botnet traffic in the future, if the security keys have unique lengths and signatures.[44] Computer security vendor Sophos has agreed with the assessment that the partitioning of the Storm botnet indicated likely resale of its services. Graham Cluley of Sophos said, "Storm's use of encrypted traffic is an interesting feature which has raised eyebrows in our lab. Its most likely use is for the cybercriminals to lease out portions of the network for misuse. It wouldn't be a surprise if the network was used for spamming, distributed denial-of-service attacks, and other malicious activities."[46] Security experts reported that if Storm is broken up for the malware market, in the form of a "ready-to-use botnet-making spam kit", the world could see a sharp rise in the number of Storm related infections and compromised computer systems.[47] The encryption only seems to affect systems compromised by Storm from the second week of October 2007 onwards, meaning that any of the computer systems compromised after that time frame will remain difficult to track and block.[48]

Within days of the discovery of this segmenting of the Storm botnet, spam e-mail from the new subsection was uncovered by major security vendors. In the evening of October 17, security vendors began seeing new spam with embedded MP3 sound files, which attempted to trick victims into investing in a penny stock, as part of an illegal pump-and-dump stock scam. It was believed that this was the first-ever spam e-mail scam that made use of audio to fool victims.[49] Unlike nearly all other Storm-related e-mails, however, these new audio stock scam messages did not include any sort of virus or Storm malware payload; they simply were part of the stock scam.[50]

In January 2008, the botnet was detected for the first time to be involved in phishing attacks against the customers of major financial institutions, targeting banking establishments in Europe including Barclays, Halifax[43] and the Royal Bank of Scotland.[51] The unique security keys used indicated to F-Secure that segments of the botnet were being leased.[51]

36.5   Claimed decline of the botnet

On September 25, 2007, it was estimated that a Microsoft update to the Windows Malicious Software Removal Tool (MSRT) may have helped reduce the size of the botnet by up to 20%.[52] The new patch, as claimed by Microsoft, removed Storm from approximately 274,372 infected systems out of 2.6 million scanned Windows systems.[53] However, according to senior security staff at Microsoft, "the 180,000+ additional machines that have been cleaned by MSRT since the first day are likely to be home user machines that were not notably incorporated into the daily operation of the 'Storm' botnet," indicating that the MSRT cleaning may have been symbolic at best.[54]

As of late October 2007, some reports indicated that the Storm botnet was losing the size of its Internet footprint, and was significantly reduced in size.[55] Brandon Enright, a University of California at San Diego security analyst, estimated that the botnet had by late October fallen to a size of approximately 160,000 compromised systems, from Enright's previous estimated high in July 2007 of 1,500,000 systems.[56] Enright noted, however, that the botnet's composition was constantly changing, and that it was still actively defending itself against attacks and observation. "If you're a researcher and you hit the pages hosting the malware too much... there is an automated process that automatically launches a denial of service [attack] against you," he said, and added that his research caused a Storm botnet attack that knocked part of the UC San Diego network

offline.[57]

The computer security company McAfee is reported as saying that the Storm Worm would be the basis of future attacks.[58] Craig Schmugar, a noted security expert who discovered the Mydoom worm, called the Storm botnet a trend-setter, which has led to more usage of similar tactics by criminals.[59] One such derivative botnet has been dubbed the "Celebrity Spam Gang", due to their use of similar technical tools as the Storm botnet controllers. Unlike the sophisticated social engineering that the Storm operators use to entice victims, however, the Celebrity spammers make use of offers of nude images of celebrities such as Angelina Jolie and Britney Spears.[60] Cisco Systems security experts stated in a report that they believe the Storm botnet would remain a critical threat in 2008, and said they estimated that its size remained in the "millions".[61]

As of early 2008, the Storm botnet also found business competition in its black hat economy, in the form of Nugache, another similar botnet which was first identified in 2006. Reports have indicated a price war may be underway between the operators of both botnets, for the sale of their spam E-mail delivery.[62] Following the Christmas and New Year's holidays bridging 2007-2008, the researchers of the German Honeynet Project reported that the Storm botnet may have increased in size by up to 20% over the holidays.[63] The *MessageLabs Intelligence* report dated March 2008 estimates that over 20% of all spam on the Internet originates from Storm.[64]

36.6   Present state of the botnet

The Storm botnet was sending out spam for more than two years until its decline in late 2008.[65] One factor in this — on account of making it less interesting for the creators to maintain the botnet — may have been the Stormfucker[66] tool, which made it possible to take control over parts of the botnet.[67]

36.7   Stormbot 2

On April 28, 2010, McAfee made an announcement that the so-called "rumors" of a Stormbot 2 were verified. Mark Schloesser, Tillmann Werner, and Felix Leder, the German researchers who did a lot of work in analyzing the original Storm, found that around two-thirds of the "new" functions are a copy and paste from the last Storm code base. The only thing missing is the P2P infrastructure, perhaps because of the tool which used P2P to bring down the original Storm. Honeynet blog dubbed this Stormbot 2.[68]

36.8   See also

- E-mail spam

- Internet crime

- Internet security

- Operation: Bot Roast

- Rustock botnet

- Botnet

- Helpful worm

- McColo

- Srizbi Botnet

- Command and control (malware)

- Zombie (computer science)

- Alureon

- Conficker

- Gameover ZeuS

- Bagle (computer worm)

- ZeroAccess botnet

- Regin (malware)

- Zeus (malware)

36.9   References

[1] Lisa Vaas (2007-10-24). "Storm Worm Botnet Lobotomizing Anti-Virus Programs". eWeek. Retrieved 4 July 2015.

[2] Spiess, Kevin (September 7, 2007). "Worm 'Storm' gathers strength". Neoseeker. Retrieved 2007-10-10.

[3] "Storm Worm's virulence may change tactics". British Computer Society. August 2, 2007. Retrieved 2007-10-10.

[4] Dvorsky, George (September 24, 2007). "Storm Botnet storms the Net". Institute for Ethics and Emerging Technologies. Retrieved 2007-10-10.

[5] Keizer, Gregg (9 April 2008). "Top botnets control 1M hijacked computers". *Computer World*. Retrieved 24 December 2012.

[6] Leyden, John (September 25, 2007). "Storm Worm retaliates against security researchers". The Register. Retrieved 2007-10-25.

[7] Gaudin, Sharon (September 18, 2007). "Storm Worm Botnet Attacks Anti-Spam Firms". InformationWeek. Retrieved 2007-10-10.

[8] Fisher, Dennis (2007-10-22). "Experts predict Storm Trojan's reign to continue". Search Security. Retrieved 2007-12-26.

[9] Coca, Rick (2007-12-18). "FBI: 'Botnets' threaten online security". Inside Bay Area. Retrieved 2007-12-27.

[10] Brodkin, Jon (September 7, 2007). "Financially motivated malware thrives". Retrieved 2007-10-10.

[11] Null, Christopher (2007-10-22). "Devastating "Storm" Computer Worm Waiting in the Wings". Yahoo! News. Retrieved 2007-12-26.

[12] Utter, David (July 13, 2007). "Storm Botnet Driving PDF Spam". Retrieved 2007-10-10.

[13] Cringely, Robert X. (October 17, 2007). "The Gathering Storm". InfoWorld.

[14] Holz, Thorsten (April 9, 2008). "Measurements and Mitigation of Peer-to-Peer-based Botnets: A Case Study on Storm Worm". Usenix. Retrieved 2008-04-23.

[15] Singel, Ryan (2007-12-07). "Report: Cybercrime Stormed the Net in 2007". Wired News. Retrieved 2007-12-27.

[16] Larkin, Erik (2007-12-03). "The Internet's Public Enemy Number One". PC World. Retrieved 2010-03-21.

[17] Gaudin, Sharon (September 6, 2007). "Storm Worm Botnet More Powerful Than Top Supercomputers". Retrieved 2007-10-10.

[18] Gaudin, Sharon (September 4, 2007). "After Short Break, Storm Worm Fires Back Up With New Tricks". InformationWeek. Retrieved 2007-10-10.

[19] Fisher, Dennis (2007-12-17). "Storm, Nugache lead dangerous new botnet barrage". Search Security. Retrieved 2007-12-27.

[20] Leyden, John (September 14, 2007). "Storm Worm linked to spam surge". The Register. Retrieved 2007-10-17.

[21] Schneier, Bruce (October 4, 2007). "Gathering 'Storm' Superworm Poses Grave Threat to PC Nets". Wired News. Retrieved 2007-10-17.

[22] Gaudin, Sharon (October 3, 2007). "Hackers Breaking Up Botnets To Elude Detection". InformationWeek. Retrieved 2007-10-17.

[23] Sorensen, Chris (October 15, 2007). "Storm Worm the 'syphilis' of computers". The Star. Retrieved 2007-10-17.

[24] Utter, David (October 16, 2007). "Storm Botnets Using Encrypted Traffic". Security Pro News. Retrieved 2007-10-17.

[25] "Storm DDoS hits anti-scam sites". Virus Bulletin.com. September 10, 2007. Retrieved 2007-10-17.

[26] Gaudin, Sharon (September 10, 2007). "NFL Kick-off Weekend Brings Another Storm Worm Attack". InformationWeek. Retrieved 2007-10-17.

[27] Hernandez, Pedro (October 4, 2007). "Storm Worm Rewrote the Botnet and Spam Game". Enterprise IT Planet. Retrieved 2007-10-17.

[28] Stewart, Joe. "Storm Worm DDoS Attack". *Secureworks.com*. SecureWorks. Retrieved 9 March 2016.

[29] McCloskey, Paul (September 14, 2007). "Storm Warning: Botnet Gearing Up To Attack Defenders". InformationWeek. Retrieved 2007-10-17.

[30] Gaudin, Sharon (September 17, 2007). "Storm botnet puts up defenses and starts attacking back". InformationWeek. Retrieved 2007-10-17.

[31] "Storm Worm offers coal for Christmas". Security Focus. 2007-12-26. Retrieved 2007-12-27.

[32] "Researchers Fear Reprisals From Storm". Dark Reading. 2007-10-29. Retrieved 2007-12-28. |first1= missing |last1= in Authors list (help)

[33] Paul, Ryan (September 12, 2007). "Spammers launch denial of service attacks against antispam sites". Ars Technica News. Retrieved 2007-10-17.

[34] Sophos Labs (2007-10-22). "Process-patching, the Dorf way". Naked security. Retrieved 4 July 2015.

[35] Farrell, Nick (September 17, 2007). "Republicans infect voters with Storm Trojan". "The Inquirer". Archived from the original on 2007-10-12. Retrieved 2007-10-17.

[36] Keizer, Gregg (September 14, 2007). "Hacked GOP Site Infects Visitors with Malware". Computerworld. Retrieved 2007-10-17.

[37] Tung, Liam (October 10, 2007). "'Storm worm' exploits YouTube". CNET News. Retrieved 2007-10-17.

[38] Keizer, Gregg (October 12, 2007). "Storm Trojan flaunts crazy cat to build out botnet". ComputerWorld. Retrieved 2007-10-17.

[39] Keizer, Gregg (2007-11-16). "Storm Botnet Spreading Malware Through GeoCities". PC World. Retrieved 2007-12-27.

[40] McMillan, Robert (2007-12-24). "Storm Worm Tempts With Christmas Strip Show". PC World. Retrieved 2007-12-27.

[41] Hruska, Joel (2007-12-25). "Storm Worm delivering coal this Christmas". Ars Technica. Retrieved 2007-12-27.

[42] Keizer, Gregg (2007-12-26). "Storm Botnet Drops Strippers Lure, Switches to New Year's". PC World. Retrieved 2007-12-27.

[43] Rogers, Jack (2008-01-08). "Fortinet: Storm Worm botnet used to mount phishing attacks on Barclays, Halifax banks". SC Magazine. Retrieved 2008-01-09.

[44] Stewart, Joe (October 15, 2007). "The Changing Storm". Secure Works. Retrieved 2007-10-17.

[45] Francia, Ruben (October 16, 2007). "Researcher: Storm Worm botnet up for sale". Tech.Blorge. Retrieved 2007-10-17.

[46] Espiner, Tom (2007-10-16). "Security expert: Storm botnet 'services' could be sold". CNet news. Retrieved 2007-10-17.

[47] Vaas, Lisa (October 16, 2007). "Storm Botnet Kits Loom on the Horizon". EWeek. Retrieved 2007-10-17.

[48] Goodin, Dan (October 15, 2007). "The balkanization of Storm Worm botnets". The Register. Retrieved 2007-10-17.

[49] Keizer, Gregg (October 18, 2007). "Spammers pump up volume with major spoken scam slam". Computerworld. Retrieved 2007-10-19.

[50] Prince, Brian (October 18, 2007). "MP3 Spam Scam Hits In-boxes". EWeek. Retrieved 2007-10-19.

[51] Vamosi, Robert (January 9, 2008). "Phishers now leasing the Storm worm botnet". CNET News. Retrieved 2008-05-11.

[52] Beskerming, Sûnnet (September 25, 2007). "Guessing at compromised host number". The Register. Retrieved 2007-10-17.

[53] Naraine, Ryan (September 24, 2007). "Storm Worm botnet numbers, via Microsoft". ZDNet. Retrieved 2007-10-17.

[54] Krebs, Brian (October 1, 2007). "Just How Bad Is the Storm Worm?". The Washington Post. Retrieved 2007-10-17.

[55] Chapman, Matt (2007-10-22). "Storm Worm may have blown itself out". VNUnet. Archived from the original on December 25, 2007. Retrieved 2007-12-26.

[56] Francia, Ruben (2007-10-21). "Storm Worm network shrinks to about one-tenth of its former size". Tech.Blorge. Retrieved 2007-12-26.

[57] McMillan, Robert (2007-10-21). "Storm Worm Now Just a Squall". PC World. Retrieved 2007-12-26.

[58] Vassou, Andrea-Marie (2007-11-29). "Cyber war to escalate in 2008". Computer Active. Retrieved 2007-12-27.

[59] Messmer, Ellen (2007-12-11). "Attackers poised to exploit Olympics, presidential elections in 2008". Network World. Retrieved 2007-12-27.

[60] "New botnet as powerful as Storm worm revealed". Secure Computing. 2007-11-29. Retrieved 2007-12-27.

[61] Rogers, Jack (2007-12-26). "Cisco reports Storm botnet may be sublet to criminals in 2008 as holiday-themed attacks proliferate". SC Magazine. Retrieved 2007-12-27.

[62] Dunn, John E. (2008-01-07). "Nugache – the next Storm?". Tech World. Retrieved 2008-01-07.

[63] Utter, David (2008-01-04). "Storm Botnet Triples In Size". Security Pro News. Retrieved 2008-01-07.

[64] "One fifth of all spam springs from Storm botnet" (PDF). *MessageLabs Intelligence: Q1 / March 2009*. MessageLabs. 2008-04-01.

[65] Felix Leder (2010-04-28). "A Breeze of Storm". *Honeynet Project Blog*. Retrieved 2010-05-24.

[66] Full Disclosure: Stormfucker

[67] Georg 'oxff' Wicherski, Tillmann Werner, Felix Leder, Mark Schlösser (2008). *Stormfucker: Owning the Storm Botnet* (Conference talk). Chaos Computer Club e.V. Retrieved 2010-05-24. Archived October 6, 2009, at the Wayback Machine.

[68] Dirro, Toralv (2010-04-28). "Dark and Stormy–Comeback of a Botnet?". McAfee Research Blog. Retrieved 2010-05-01.

36.10   External links

- A video released by Secure Labs, showing the spread of the botnet on YouTube

- "The Storm worm: can you be certain your machine isn't infected?" The target page is no longer on this website.

- "TrustedSource Storm Tracker": Top Storm domains and latest web proxies The target page is no longer on this website.

Chapter 37

Torpig

Torpig, also known as **Sinowal** or **Anserin** is a type of botnet spread through systems compromised by the Mebroot rootkit by a variety of trojan horses for the purpose of collecting sensitive personal and corporate data such as bank account and credit card information. It targets computers that use Microsoft Windows, recruiting a network of zombies for the botnet. Torpig circumvents antivirus software through the use of rootkit technology and scans the infected system for credentials, accounts and passwords as well as potentially allowing attackers full access to the computer. It is also purportedly capable of modifying data on the computer, and can perform man-in-the-browser attacks.

By November 2008, it was estimated that Torpig had stolen the details of about 500,000 online bank accounts and credit and debit cards and was described as "one of the most advanced pieces of crimeware ever created".[1]

37.1 History

Torpig reportedly began development in 2005, evolving from that point to more effectively evade detection by the host system and antivirus software.[2]

In early 2009, a team of security researchers from University of California, Santa Barbara took control of the botnet for ten days. During that time, they extracted an unprecedented amount (over 70 GB) of stolen data and redirected 1.2 million IPs on to their private command and control server. The report[3] goes into great detail about how the botnet operates. During the UCSB research team's ten-day takeover of the botnet, Torpig was able to retrieve login information for 8,310 accounts at 410 different institutions, and 1,660 unique credit and debit card numbers from victims in the U.S. (49%), Italy (12%), Spain (8%), and 40 other countries, including cards from Visa (1,056), MasterCard (447), American Express (81), Maestro (36), and Discover (24).[4]

37.2 Operation

Initially, a great deal of Torpig's spread was attributable to phishing emails that tricked users into installing the malicious software. More sophisticated delivery methods developed since that time use malicious banner ads which take advantage of exploits found in outdated of versions of Java, or Adobe Acrobat, Flash, Shockwave. A type of Drive-by download, this method typically does not require the user to click on the ad, and the download may commence without any visible indications after the malicious ad recognizes the old software version and redirects the browser to the Torpig download site. To complete its installation into the infected computer's Master Boot Record (MBR), the trojan will restart the computer.[2]

During the main stage of the infection, the malware will upload information from the computer twenty minutes at a time, including financial data like credit card numbers and credentials for banking accounts, as well as e-mail accounts, Windows passwords, FTP credentials, and POP/SMTP accounts.[4]

37.3 See also

- Mebroot
- Drive-by download
- Phishing
- Man-in-the-browser
- Conficker a worm that also uses domain name generation (or domain flux)
- Timeline of computer viruses and worms

37.4 References

[1] BBC News: Trojan virus steals bank info

[2] Carnegie Mellon University. "Torpig". Archived from the original on 19 May 2015. Retrieved 25 July 2015.

[3] UCSB Torpig report

[4] Naraine, Ryan (4 May 2009). "Botnet hijack: Inside the Torpig malware operation". ZDNet. Archived from the original on 1 August 2015. Retrieved 1 August 2015.

37.5 External links

- UCSB Analysis

- One Sinowal Trojan + One Gang = Hundreds of Thousands of Compromised Accounts by RSA FraudAction Research Lab, October 2008

- Don't be a victim of Sinowal, the super-Trojan by Woody Leonhard, WindowsSecrets.com, November 2008

- Antivirus tools try to remove Sinowal/Mebroot by Woody Leonhard, WindowsSecrets.com, November 2008

- Taking over the Torpig botnet, IEEE, Jan/Feb 2011

- Torpig Botnet Hijacked and Dissected covered on Slashdot, May 2009

- How to Steal a Botnet and What Can Happen When You Do by Richard A. Kemmerer, GoogleTechTalks, September 2009

Chapter 38

Tribe Flood Network

The **Tribe Flood Network** or **TFN** is a set of computer programs to conduct various DDoS attacks such as ICMP flood, SYN flood, UDP flood and Smurf attack.

First **TFN** initiated attacks are described in CERT Incident Note 99-04.

TFN2K was written by Mixter, a security professional and hacker based in Germany.

38.1   See also

- Stacheldraht

- Trinoo

- High Orbit Ion Cannon

- Low Orbit Ion Cannon

38.2   External links

- Tribe Flood Network

- TFN2K - An Analysis by Jason Barlow and Woody Thrower of AXENT Security Team

- TFN2K source code

Chapter 39

Trinoo

The **trinoo** or **trin00** is a set of computer programs to conduct a DDoS attack. It is believed that **trinoo** networks have been set up on thousands of systems on the Internet that have been compromised by remote buffer overrun exploits.[1]

The first suspected **trinoo** attacks are described in CERT Incident Note 99-04.[2] A trinoo network has been connected to the February 2000 distributed denial of service attack on the Yahoo! website.[3]

Trinoo is famous for allowing attackers to leave a message in a folder called **cry_baby**. The file is self replicating and is modified on a regular basis as long as port 80 is active.

39.1 Using Trinoo

39.1.1 Step 1

The attacker, using a compromised host, compiles a list of machines that can be compromised. Most of this process is done automatically from the compromised host, because the host stores a mount of information including how to find other hosts to compromise.

39.1.2 Step 2

As soon as the list of machines that can be compromised has been compiled, scripts are run to compromise them and convert them into the Trinoo Masters or Daemons. One Master can control multiple Daemons. The Daemons are the compromised hosts that launch the actual UDP floods against the victim machine.

39.1.3 Step 3

The DDoS attack is launched when the attacker issues a command on the Master hosts. The Masters instruct every Daemon to start a DoS attack against the IP address specified in the command, many DoSs comprise the DDoS attack.

39.2 See also

- Stacheldraht
- Tribe Flood Network
- High Orbit Ion Cannon
- Low Orbit Ion Cannon

39.3 References

[1] http://staff.washington.edu/dittrich/misc/trinoo.analysis

[2] In case the URL for that ("the original") is a dead link -- which was seen on July 27, 2014 -- there is an "archived" copy of CERT® Incident Note IN-99-04 still online, as follows: "CERT® Incident Note IN-99-04". CERT. April 1999. Archived from the original on October 16, 2009. Retrieved July 27, 2014.

[3] Sinrod, Eric J.; William P. Reilly (May 2000). "Cyber Crimes: A Practical Approach to the Application of Federal Computer Crime Laws" (PDF 235 KB). *Santa Clara Computer and High Technology Law Journal*. California: Santa Clara University School of Law. **16** (2): 17. ISSN 0882-3383. Retrieved 2008-11-04.

39.4 External links

- Trinoo description by Symantec
- Trinoo Analysis by David Dittrich
- Trinoo source code

Chapter 40

United States v. Ancheta

United States of America v. Ancheta (U.S. vs. Ancheta, 06-051 (C.D. Cal.)) is the name of a lawsuit against Jeanson James Ancheta of Downey, California by the U.S. Government and was handled by the United States District Court for the Central District of California . This is the first botnet related prosecution in U.S history.

40.1 Case summary

Ancheta violated the prohibited acts of accessing and transmitting malware with the intent and consequence of disrupting interstate and foreign commerce. The case was the first prosecution in the United States of America where an individual was sentenced to prison for profiting from the use of botnets that were used maliciously to launch destructive denial of service attacks and sending of large quantities of spam across the internet. The 57-month prison sentence for Ancheta was the longest in history for a defendant who has spread malware.

Ancheta pleaded guilty to conspiring to violate to the Computer Fraud and Abuse Act causing damage to computers used by the federal government of the United States in national defence and accessing a protected computer without authorization for the purpose of commit various types of fraud. Between the dates of June 25, 2004 and September 15, 2004 in Los Angeles county Ancheta and others knowingly conspired to violate 18 U.S.C. § 1030(a)(5)(A)(i), 18 U.S.C. § 1030(a)(5)(B)(i) and 18 U.S.C. § 1030(b) of US Code. This refers to knowingly causing the transmission of a program, information, code or command and as a result of such conduct cause damage without authorization to a computer used in interstate and foreign commerce and communication and cause loss during a one-year period aggregating at least $5000 in value. Secondly Acheta and others conspired to violate 18 U.S.C. § 1037(a)(1), 18 U.S.C. § 1037(b)(2)(A), and 18 U.S.C. § 1037(b)(2)(F) of US Code. This refers to access without authorization a computer used in interstate and foreign commerce and communication, and intentionally intimate the transmission from and through that computer multiple commercial electronic email messages that affect interstate and foreign commerce. Finally Ancheta was charged for laundering of monetary instruments under 18 U.S.C. § 1956(a)(1)(A)(i) and faced criminal forfeiture under 18 U.S.C. § 982 and 21 U.S.C. § 853.

40.2 Case technical details

40.2.1 Interent bots and botnets

Jeanson James Ancheta at the time of this crime was a 20-year-old high school drop-out. He found the rxbot software online and decided that he was going to use it to create a botnet army. Once established, he set up a website where he would rent his computer zombies to hackers so that they could employ them to fulfill whatever malicious job they had planned. Ancheta used at least one computer system at his place of residence and accessed the Internet from a dial up telephone line to configure and command the botnet and conduct any business communication. A co-conspirator residing in Boca Raton, Florida referred to as SoBE was also involved, as he had previous experience launching computer attacks.

An internet bot is a program that infects a computer and enables remote control of that computer.[1] A security vulnerability in the computer system is exploited by the hacker in order to install and run the malware; in this case a worm. The program installs itself and is set up to run as a background process or daemon which remains undetectable to the computer user. The infected computer is often referred to as a zombie computer and was what Ancheta depended on as the building block of his botnet army. Ancheta engaged these computers to function in unison in a network formation; this is referred to as a botnet and the controller is called the bot herder. Ancheta's primary purpose of engaging large numbers of computers was to amplify the attack and reduce the time taken to execute it. Their greatest value is they provide a relatively high level of anonymity.[2]

In 2005, the Federal Trade Commission in conjunction with 35 government agencies organized an initiative to encourage Internet service providers to actively monitor, identify and quarantine customers whose computers appeared to have been compromised, transformed into zombies, or appear to be under the remote control of hackers.[3] One of the largest botnet implementations around that time (2005) was found by Dutch Police where a botnet of over 1.5 million computers was under a crime ring's control.[4] These zombie computers were often employed as a response to anti-spam laws and spam filtering. Spammers started hiring virus writers and hackers to help them architect armies of zombie computers to send spam email from unsuspecting users' computers around the world.[5] In February 2012, the Federal Communications Commission unveiled yet another plan that calls on Internet service providers to take specific steps to combat online threats from botnets.[6]

40.2.2 IRC setup and worm development

In July 2004 Ancheta obtained access to a server from an internet hosting company, set it up as an IRC Server utilizing the IRCd program, and created a channel on IRC which he controlled remotely. Ancheta developed a computer worm which when installed and executed would report back to the IRC channel he controlled, scan for other computers with similar vulnerabilities, and leave itself open itself up for future unauthorized control. Ancheta initially developed this worm by modifying an existing Trojan called rxbot. While DDOS attacks were one use case for these botnets, another major purpose was to use them as a proxy server for email spam propagation. In 2004 it was reported that unsolicited email had doubled from late 2003, rising from 310 billion message to 700 billion messages.[7] Worms like Conficker originally found in 2008 still remain a threat and is significantly more sophisticated, disallowing updates and communicated through encrypted channels.[8]

40.2.3 Profiting

Ancheta advertised the sale of bots for the purpose of launching distributed denial-of-service (DDoS) attacks or to send spam. He sold access to the bots in clusters, usually up to 10,000 at a time. Ancheta acted as a consultant and advised the buyer on the exact number of bots they would need to successfully accomplish the designated attack. He would offer separate channels for an additional cost to assist in the control and direction of the bots, providing temporary control over the channel to the buyer. Around the time of this crime, it was estimated that an average botnet was 20,000 computers in size.[9] He also profited from sale of the developed worm which he would configure for

best propagation. Buyers also had the option of using their own malware to launch the attack and not use the worm he was offering. Ancheta accepted all payments through Paypal, where he would misleadingly describe the nature of the transaction as hosting, web hosting, or dedicated box services.

40.3 Case legal details

In total there were 17 different counts in this case.

40.3.1 Conspiracy to commit an offense or defraud a US agency

Count 1 was in violation of 18 U.S.C. § 371. This refers to the conspiracy between Ancheta and others to commit an offense or to defraud a US agency. This violated 18 U.S.C. § 1030(a)(5)(A)(i), 18 U.S.C. § 1030(a)(5)(B)(i) and 18 U.S.C. § 1030(b) of US Code.

40.3.2 Fraud and related activity in connection with computers

Counts 2 through 11 were in violation of 18 U.S.C. § 1030(a)(5)(A)(i), 18 U.S.C. § 1030(a)(5)(B)(v) and 18 U.S.C. § 1030(b)

Counts 2, 3 and 4 involved intentionally causing damage while accessing an unauthorized computer belonging to King Pao Electronic Co and Sanyo Electric Software which if completed would have caused damage exceeding $5000 and launching a distributed denial of service (DDOS) attack to a company (whose name remains confidential) which if completed would have caused damage exceeding $5000. In furtherance of the conspiracy Ancheta committed various overt acts, including payments to accomplices, directing numerous computers to adware servers controlled by Ancheta himself. These servers were where unsuspecting users would be redirected to download the malware. Counts 5 and 6 included knowingly causing the transmission of malicious code to protected computers belonging to the Naval Air Weapons Station China Lake and the US Defense Information Systems Agency; both used for justice, national defence, and national security. NAWS China Lake is a major Navy research, testing and evaluation facility and DISA provides IT and communication support the President and other top executive staff of the US Government.

Count 7 through 11 were in violation of 18 U.S.C. § 1030(a)(4) and 18 U.S.C. § 1030(b). Ancheta knowingly accessed without authorization, computers involved in interstate and foreign commerce by installing adware without notice, or consent with the sole intent to defraud. Between 8,744 and 53,321 computers (different for each count) were accessed without authorization and monetary amounts between $1306.52 and 7966.10 (different for each count) accepted as payment for services.

40.3.3   Laundering of monetary instruments

Counts 12 through 16 were in violation of 18 U.S.C. § 1956(a)(1)(A)(i). Knowing that property involved in a financial transaction represents the proceeds of some unlawful activity, Ancheta conducted financial transactions that involved the proceeds of specified unlawful activity and those proceeds were further used with the intent to promote more unlawful activity. Proceeds from selling worms and the rental of the botnet were being passed as legitimate online transactions such as payments for web hosting or dedicated box services. Anchta was also transferring the same payments to internet hosting companies for additional access to the servers used to commit further fraud. From November 2004 to May 2005 varying amounts of funds were transferred from Wells Fargo Bank to FDCServers and Sago Networks.

40.3.4   Criminal forfeiture

Count 17 was in violation of 18 U.S.C. § 982 and 21 U.S.C. § 853. Ancheta was required to forfeit all property involved in the offence. This included $2998.81 generated from the sale of internet bots and proxies and deposited into a Wells Fargo account, approximately $58,357.86 in proceeds generated from the surreptitious install of adware on protected computers linked to a Paypal account owned by Ancheta, a 1993 BMW 325 IS, and all property used to commit or facilitate the commission of the above violations including desktop computers, laptops and hard drives.

40.4   Summary of laws applied

- 18 U.S.C. § 371: Conspiracy to commit offense or to defraud United States

- 21 U.S.C. § 853: Criminal Forfeiture

- 18 U.S.C. § 982: Criminal Forfeiture

- 18 U.S.C. § 1037(a)(1): Fraud and related activity in connection with email

- 18 U.S.C. § 1037(b)(2)(A): Fraud and related activity in connection with email

- 18 U.S.C. § 1037(b)(2)(F): Fraud and related activity in connection with email

- 18 U.S.C. § 1030(a)(3): Computer trespassing in a government computer

- 18 U.S.C. § 1030(a)(4): Committing fraud with a protected computer

- 18 U.S.C. § 1030(a)(5)(A)(i): Damaging a protected computer (including viruses, worms)

- 18 U.S.C. § 1030(a)(5)(B)(i): Damaging a [protected computer (including viruses, worms)

- 18 U.S.C. § 1030(b): Conspiracy to violate (a)

- 18 U.S.C. § 1956(a)(1)(A)(i): Laundering of monetary instruments

40.5   See also

- Computer crime

- Computer worm

- Computer Fraud and Abuse Act

40.6   References

[1] "Botnet (Zombie Army)". TechTarget. December 2004.

[2] McMillian, Robert (September 19, 2005). "Zombie Armies Attack British PCs". PCWorld.

[3] Leyden, John (May 24, 2005). "ISPs urged to throttle spam zombies". The Register.

[4] Sanders, Tom (October 21, 2005). "Botnet operation controlled 1.5m PCs". Incisive Media.

[5] Spring, Tom (June 20, 2005). "Spam Slayer: Slaying Spam-Spewing Zombie PCs". PCWorld.

[6] Albanesius, Chloe (February 22, 2012). "FCC Pushes ISPs to Fight Botnets, Other Cyber-Security Threats". PC Magazine.

[7] Ray, Tiernan (February 18, 2004). "E-Mail viruses blamed as spam rises sharply". The Seattle Times.

[8] Emspak, Jesse (January 27, 2001). "Years-old Confiker Worm Still A Threat". IBTimes.

[9] Garber, Lee (April 2006). "Hackers Strengthen Malicious Botnets By Shrinking Them" (PDF). *Computer*. IEEE Computer Society. **39** (April 2006): 19. doi:10.1109/MC.2006.136.

40.7 External links

- Text of the decision

- US Department of Justice - Ancheta Case

- Wired.com How-to: Build your own botnet with open source software

Chapter 41

Virut

Virut is a cybercrime malware botnet, operating at least since 2006, and one of the major botnets and malware distributors on the Internet. In January 2013 its operations were disrupted by the Polish organization Naukowa i Akademicka Sieć Komputerowa.

41.1 Characteristics

Virut is a malware botnet that is known to be used for cybercrime activities such as DDoS attacks, spam (in collaboration with the Waledac botnet[1]), fraud, data theft, and pay-per-install activities.[2][3][4] It spreads through executable file infection (through infected USB sticks and other media), and more recently, through compromised HTML files (thus infecting vulnerable browsers visiting compromised websites).[2][5] It has infected computers associated with at least 890,000 IP addresses in Poland.[2] In 2012, Symantec estimated that the botnet had control of over 300,000 computers worldwide, primarily in Egypt, Pakistan and Southeast Asia (including India).[2][3] A Kaspersky report listed Virut as the fifth-most widespread threat in the third quarter of 2012, responsible for 5.5% of computer infections.[2][6]

41.2 History

The Virut botnet has been active since at least 2006.[2]

On 17 January 2013, Polish research and development organization, data networks operator, and the operator of the Polish ".pl" top-level domain registry, Naukowa i Akademicka Sieć Komputerowa (NASK), took over twenty three domains used by Virut to attempt to shut it down.[2] A NASK spokesperson stated that it was the first time NASK engaged in such an operation (taking over domains), owing to the major threat that the Virut botnet posed to the Internet.[5] It is likely Virut will not be shut down completely, as some of its control servers are located at Russian ".ru" top-level domain name registrars outside the reach of the Polish NASK.[4] Further, the botnet is able to look up alternate backup hosts, enabling the criminals operating it to reestablish control over the network.[4]

41.3 See also

- Command and control (malware)
- Zombie (computer science)
- Trojan horse (computing)
- Botnet
- Alureon
- Conficker
- Gameover ZeuS
- ZeroAccess botnet
- Regin (malware)
- Zeus (malware)
- Timeline of computer viruses and worms

41.4 References

[1] "Waledac Malware Could Send 3.6 Billion Spam Emails per Day from Infected PCs - Softpedia". News.softpedia.com. 2013-01-15. Retrieved 2013-01-19.

[2] "CERT Polska » Blog Archive » NASK shuts down dangerous Virut botnet domains". Cert.pl. Retrieved 2013-01-19.

[3] "Snapshot of Virut Botnet After Interruption | Symantec Connect Community". Symantec.com. 2013-01-07. Retrieved 2013-01-19.

[4] "Polish Takedown Targets 'Virut' Botnet — Krebs on Security". Krebsonsecurity.com. 2013-01-07. Retrieved 2013-01-19.

[5] "•• Przejęto niebezpieczne domeny botnetu Virut | NASK odnosi sukces w walce z cyberzagrożeniami |". Komputer-swiat.pl. 1972-02-08. Retrieved 2013-01-19.

[6] "Kaspersky Security Bulletin 2012. The overall statistics for 2012". Securelist. 2012-12-10. Retrieved 2013-01-19.

Chapter 42

Vulcanbot

Vulcanbot is the name of a botnet predominantly spread in Vietnam. The botnet began to spread after the website of the Vietnamese Professionals Society (vps.org) was hacked and the legitimate Vietnamese keyboard driver (VPSKeys) hosted on the site was replaced with a backdoored version. Google posted on its blog that it believed the botnet thus created was used predominantly to DDoS bloggers critical of the bauxite mining in Vietnam, thus making it a politically motivated attack.[1]

42.1   See also

- Operation Aurora

42.2   References

[1] http://www.theregister.co.uk/2010/03/31/vietnam_botnet/

Chapter 43

Waledac botnet

Waledac, also known by its aliases **Waled** and **Waled-pak**,[1] was a botnet mostly involved in e-mail spam and malware. In March 2010 the botnet was taken down by Microsoft.[2][3]

43.1 Operations

Before its eventual takedown, the Waledac botnet consisted of an estimated 70,000-90,000 computers infected with the "Waledac" computer worm.[2] The botnet itself was capable of sending about 1.5 billion spam messages a day, or about 1% of the total global spam volume.[3][4]

On February 25, 2010, Microsoft won a court order which resulted in the temporal cut-off of 277 domain names which were being used as command and control servers for the botnet, effectively crippling a large part of the botnet.[5] However, besides operating through command and control servers the Waledac worm is also capable of operating through peer-to-peer communication between the various botnet nodes, which means that the extent of the damage is difficult to measure.[6] Codenamed 'Operation b49', an investigation was conducted for some months which thereby yielded an end to the 'zombie' computers. More than a million 'zombie' computers were brought out of the garrison of the hackers but still infected.[7]

In early September 2010, Microsoft was granted ownership of the 277 domains used by Waledac to broadcast spam email.[8]

43.2 See also

- Botnet
- Internet crime
- Internet security
- Command and control (malware)

- Zombie (computer science)

43.3 References

[1] "Waledac". M86 Security. 2009-04-20. Retrieved 2010-07-30.

[2] Goodin, Dan (2010-03-16). "Waledac botnet 'decimated' by MS takedown; Up to 90,000 zombies freed". *theregister.co.uk*. London, UK: The Register. Retrieved 2014-01-09.

[3] Whitney, Lance (2010-02-25). "With legal nod, Microsoft ambushes Waledac botnet | Security - CNET News". News.cnet.com. Retrieved 2010-07-30.

[4] Claburn, Thomas. "Microsoft Decapitates Waledac Botnet". InformationWeek. Retrieved 2010-07-30.

[5] Leyden, John (2010-02-25). "MS uses court order to take out Waledac botnet; Zombie network decapitated. For now". *theregister.co.uk*. London, UK: The Register. Retrieved 2014-01-09.

[6] "Waledac Botnet - Deployment & Communication Analysis". FortiGuard. 2009-09-30. Retrieved 2010-07-30.

[7] Help Net Security. "Microsoft cripples the Waledac botnet". Net-security.org. Retrieved 2014-01-09.

[8] Acohido, Byron (2010-09-08). "Microsoft gets legal might to target spamming botnets". *USA Today*.

43.4 External links

- Technical analysis of the Waledac worm
- Is the infamous Waledac botnet out of the picture or not? | TechRepublic.com

Chapter 44

Xor DDoS

XOR DDoS is Trojan malware that hijacks Linux systems and uses them to launch DDoS attacks which have reached loads of 150+ Gbps.[1] In order to gain access it launches a brute force attack in order to discover the password to Secure Shell services on Linux.[2] Once Secure Shell credentials are acquired and login is successful, it uses root privileges to run a script that downloads and installs XOR DDoS.[3] It appears to attack targets mostly based in Asia and is also believed to be of Asian origin based on its targets(which are tend to be located in Asia.). [4] Several things are noteworthy about XOR DDoS, such as that it is built exclusively for ARM and x86 systems and it appears to have been programmed in C/C++. [5]

44.1   See also

- Application layer DDoS attack
- Botnet
- Command and control (malware)
- Dendroid (Malware)
- Denial-of-service attack
- Rootkit
- Zombie (computer science)
- ZeroAccess botnet

44.2   References

[1] "XOR DDoS Botnet Launching 20 Attacks a Day From Compromised Linux Machines | Akamai". akamai.com. Retrieved 2016-03-18.

[2] "New Botnet Hunts for Linux — Launching 20 DDoS Attacks/Day at 150Gbps". thehackernews.com. Retrieved 2016-03-18.

[3] Reuters Editorial.   "http://www.reuters.com/article/akamai-ddos-advisory-idUSnPn5TLPMJ+9f+PRN20150929".   reuters.com.   Retrieved 2016-03-18. External link in |title= (help)

[4] "Threat Advisory: XOR DDoS | DDoS mitigation, YARA, Snort". stateoftheinternet.com. Retrieved 2016-03-18.

[5] "Anatomy of a Brute Force Campaign: The Story of Hee Thai Limited « Threat Research Blog | FireEye Inc". web.archive.org. Retrieved 2016-03-18.

-
-
-
-

Chapter 45

ZeroAccess botnet

ZeroAccess is a Trojan horse computer malware that affects Microsoft Windows operating systems. It is used to download other malware on an infected machine from a botnet mostly involved in bitcoin mining and click fraud, while remaining hidden on a system using rootkit techniques.[1]

45.1 History and propagation

The ZeroAccess botnet was discovered at least around May 2011.[2] The ZeroAccess rootkit responsible for the botnet's spread is estimated to have been present on at least 9 million systems.[3] Estimates of the size of the botnet vary across sources; antivirus vendor Sophos estimated the botnet size at around 1 million active and infected machines in the third quarter of 2012, and security firm Kindsight estimated 2.2 million infected and active systems.[4][5]

The bot itself is spread through the ZeroAccess rootkit through a variety of attack vectors. One attack vector is a form of social engineering, where a user is persuaded to execute malicious code either by disguising it as a legitimate file, or including it hidden as an additional payload in an executable which announces itself as, for example, by-passing copyright protection (a keygen). A second attack vector utilizes an advertising network in order to have the user click on an advertisement that redirects them to a site hosting the malicious software itself. A third infection vector used is an affiliate scheme where third party persons are paid for installing the rootkit on a system.[6][7]

In December 2013 a coalition led by Microsoft moved to destroy the command and control network for the botnet. The attack was ineffective though because not all C&C were seized, and its peer-to-peer command and control component was unaffected - meaning the botnet could still be updated at will.[8]

45.2 Operation

Once a system has been infected with the ZeroAccess rootkit it will start one of the two main botnet operations: bitcoin mining or Click fraud. Machines involved in bitcoin mining generate bitcoins for their controller, the estimated worth of which was estimated at 2.7 million US dollars per year in September 2012.[9] The machines used for click fraud simulate clicks on website advertisements paid for on a pay per click basis. The estimated profit for this activity may be as high as 100,000 US dollars per day,[10][11] costing advertisers $900,000 a day in fraudulent clicks.[12] Typically, ZeroAccess infects the Master Boot Record (MBR) of the infected machine. It may alternatively infect a random driver in C:\Windows\System32\Drivers giving it total control over the operating system. It also disables the Windows Security Center, Firewall, and Windows Defender from the operating system. ZeroAccess also hooks itself into the tcp/ip stack to help with the Click fraud.

45.3 See also

- Botnet
- Malware
- Command and control (malware)
- Zombie (computer science)
- Internet crime
- Internet security
- Click fraud
- Clickbot.A

45.4 References

[1] https://www.symantec.com/security_response/writeup.jsp?docid=2011-071314-0410-99

[2] Monthly Malware Statistics, May 2011 (*Securelist*)

[3] Wyke, James (September 19, 2012). "Over 9 million PCs infected – ZeroAccess botnet uncovered". *Sophos*. Retrieved 27 December 2012.

[4] Jackson Higgins, Kelly (Oct 30, 2012). "ZeroAccess Botnet Surges". *Dark Reading*. Archived from the original on 2012-12-03. Retrieved 27 December 2012.

[5] Kumar, Mohit (19 Sep 2012). "9 million PCs infected with ZeroAccess botnet - Hacker News , Security updates". *The hacker news*. Retrieved 27 December 2012.

[6] Wyke, James. "The ZeroAccess rootkit". *Sophos*. p. 2. Retrieved 27 December 2012.

[7] Mimoso, Michael (October 30, 2012). "ZeroAccess Botnet Cashing in on Click Fraud and Bitcoin Mining". *ThreatPost*. Archived from the original on 2012-12-03. Retrieved 27 December 2012.

[8] Gallagher, Sean (6 December 2013). "Microsoft disrupts botnet that generated $2.7M per month for operators". *Ars Technica*. Retrieved 9 December 2013.

[9] Wyke, James. "The ZeroAccess Botnet: Mining and Fraud for Massive Financial Gain" (PDF). *Sophos*. pp. (Page 45). Retrieved 27 December 2012.

[10] Leyden, John (24 September 2012). "Crooks can milk '$100k a day' from 1-million-zombie ZeroAccess army". *The Register*. Retrieved 27 December 2012.

[11] Ragan, Steve (October 31, 2012). "Millions of Home Networks Infected by ZeroAccess Botnet". *SecurityWeek*. Retrieved 27 December 2012.

[12] Dunn, John E (2 November 2012). "ZeroAccess bot has infected 2 million consumers, firm calculates". *Techworld*. Retrieved 27 December 2012.

45.5   External links

- Analysis of the ZeroAccess botnet, created by Sophos.

- ZeroAccess Botnet, Kindsight Security Labs.

- New C&C Protocol for ZeroAccess, Kindsight Security Labs.

Chapter 46

Zeus (malware)

"Zbot" redirects here. For the action figures, see Zbots. For other uses, see Zeus (disambiguation). Not to be confused with Gameover ZeuS.

Zeus, ZeuS, or Zbot is a Trojan horse malware package that runs on versions of Microsoft Windows. While it can be used to carry out many malicious and criminal tasks, it is often used to steal banking information by man-in-the-browser keystroke logging and form grabbing. It is also used to install the CryptoLocker ransomware.[1] Zeus is spread mainly through drive-by downloads and phishing schemes. First identified in July 2007 when it was used to steal information from the United States Department of Transportation,[2] it became more widespread in March 2009. In June 2009 security company Prevx discovered that Zeus had compromised over 74,000 FTP accounts on websites of such companies as the Bank of America, NASA, Monster.com, ABC, Oracle, Play.com, Cisco, Amazon, and *BusinessWeek*.[3] Similarly to Koobface, Zeus has also been used to trick victims of tech support scams into giving the scam artists money through pop-up messages that claim the user has a virus, when in reality they might have no viruses at all. The scammers may use programs such as Command prompt or Event viewer to make the user believe that their computer is infected.[4]

46.1 Detection and removal

Zeus is very difficult to detect even with up-to-date antivirus and other security software as it hides itself using stealth techniques.[5] It is considered that this is the primary reason why the Zeus malware has become the largest botnet on the Internet: Damballa estimated that the malware infected 3.6 million PCs in the U.S. in 2009.[6] Security experts are advising that businesses continue to offer training to users to teach them to not to click on hostile or suspicious links in emails or Web sites, and to keep antivirus protection up to date. Antivirus software does not claim to reliably prevent infection; for example Browser Protection says that it can

prevent "some infection attempts".[7]

46.2 FBI crackdown

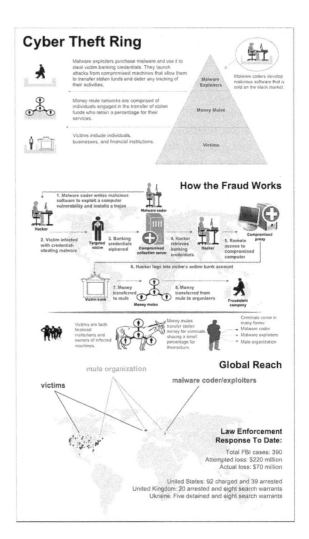

FBI: The Zeus Fraud Scheme

In October 2010 the US FBI announced that hackers in

Eastern Europe had managed to infect computers around the world using Zeus.[8] The virus was distributed in an e-mail, and when targeted individuals at businesses and municipalities opened the e-mail, the trojan software installed itself on the victimized computer, secretly capturing passwords, account numbers, and other data used to log in to online banking accounts.

The hackers then used this information to take over the victims' bank accounts and make unauthorized transfers of thousands of dollars at a time, often routing the funds to other accounts controlled by a network of money mules, paid a commission. Many of the U.S. money mules were recruited from overseas. They created bank accounts using fake documents and false names. Once the money was in the accounts, the mules would either wire it back to their bosses in Eastern Europe, or withdraw it in cash and smuggle it out of the country.[9]

More than 100 people were arrested on charges of conspiracy to commit bank fraud and money laundering, over 90 in the US, and the others in the UK and Ukraine.[10] Members of the ring had stolen $70 million.

In 2013 Hamza Bendelladj, known as Bx1 online, was arrested in Thailand [11] and deported to Atlanta, Georgia, USA. Early reports said that he was the mastermind behind ZeuS. He was accused of operating SpyEye (a bot functionally similar to ZeuS) botnets, and suspected of also operating ZeuS botnets. He was charged with several counts of wire fraud and computer fraud and abuse.[12] Court papers allege that from 2009 to 2011 Bendelladj and others "developed, marketed and sold various versions of the SpyEye virus and component parts on the Internet and allowed cybercriminals to customize their purchases to include tailor-made methods of obtaining victims' personal and financial information". It was also alleged that Bendelladj advertised SpyEye on Internet forums devoted to cyber- and other crimes and operated Command and Control servers.[13] The charges in Georgia relate only to SpyEye, as a SpyEye botnet control server was based in Atlanta.

46.3 Possible retirement of creator

In late 2010, a number of Internet security vendors including McAfee and Internet Identity claimed that the creator of Zeus had said that he was retiring and had given the source code and rights to sell Zeus to his biggest competitor, the creator of the SpyEye trojan. However, those same experts warned the retirement was a ruse and expect the developer to return with new tricks.[14][15]

46.4 See also

- Conficker

- Command and control (malware)

- Gameover ZeuS, the successor to ZeuS

- Operation Tovar

- Timeline of computer viruses and worms

- Tiny Banker Trojan

- Torpig

- Zombie (computer science)

46.5 References

[1] Abrams, Lawrence. "CryptoLocker Ransomware Information Guide and FAQ". *Bleeping Computer*. Retrieved 25 October 2013.

[2] Jim Finkle (17 July 2007). "Hackers steal U.S. government, corporate data from PCs". *Reuters*. Retrieved 17 November 2009.

[3] Steve Ragan (29 June 2009). "ZBot data dump discovered with over 74,000 FTP credentials". *The Tech Herald*. Retrieved 17 November 2009.

[4] "How to Recognize a Fake Virus Warning". Retrieved 2016-07-28.

[5] "ZeuS Banking Trojan Report". Dell SecuWorks. Retrieved 2 March 2016.

[6] "The Hunt for the Financial Industry's Most-Wanted Hacker". Bloomberg Business. Retrieved 2 March 2016.

[7] "Trojan.Zbot". Symantec. Retrieved 19 February 2010.

[8] "Cyber Banking Fraud". The Federal Bureau of Investigation. Retrieved 2 March 2016.

[9] FBI (1 October 2010). "CYBER BANKING FRAUD Global Partnerships Lead to Major Arrests". Archived from the original on 3 October 2010. Retrieved 2 October 2010.

[10] BBC (1 October 2010). "More than 100 arrests, as FBI uncovers cyber crime ring". *BBC News*. Retrieved 2 October 2010.

[11] Al Jazeera (21 September 2015). "Hamza Bendelladj: Is the Algerian hacker a hero?". *AJE News*. Retrieved 21 March 2016.

[12] Zetter, Kim. "Alleged 'SpyEye' Botmaster Ends Up in America, Handcuffs, Kim Zetter, Wired, 3 May 2013". Wired.com. Retrieved 2014-01-30.

[13] "Alleged "SpyEye" mastermind extradited to US, Lisa Vaas, 7 May 2013, Sophos nakedsecurity". Nakedsecurity.sophos.com. 2013-05-07. Retrieved 2014-01-30.

[14] Diane Bartz (29 October 2010). "Top hacker "retires"; experts brace for his return". *Reuters*. Retrieved 16 December 2010.

[15] Internet Identity (6 December 2010). "Growth in Social Networking, Mobile and Infrastructure Attacks Threaten Corporate Security in 2011". *Yahoo! Finance*. Retrieved 16 December 2010.

46.6   External links

- "Measuring the in-the-wild effectiveness of Antivirus against Zeus" Study by Internet security firm Trusteer.

- "A summary of the ZeuS Bot" A summary of ZeuS as a Trojan and Botnet, plus vector of attacks.

- "The Kneber BotNet" by Alex Cox NetWitness Whitepaper on the Kneber botnet.

- "België legt fraude met onlinebankieren bloot" Dutch news article about a banking trojan

- "Indications in affected systems" Files and registry keys created by different versions of Zeus Trojan.

- Zeus, le dieu des virus contre les banques (French)

- Zeus Bot's User Guide

- Zeus source code at GitHub

- Botnet Bust - SpyEye Malware Mastermind Pleads Guilty, FBI

46.7 Text and image sources, contributors, and licenses

46.7.1 Text

- **Botnet** *Source:* https://en.wikipedia.org/wiki/Botnet?oldid=743609864 *Contributors:* The Anome, Fubar Obfusco, Jtk, DonDaMon, Edward, Pnm, Baylink, Plop, Dean p foster, Julesd, Dynabee, Kaihsu, Pedant17, Furrykef, Dimadick, Tbutzon, Walloon, Alerante, Gtrmp, Rick Block, Gracefool, Khalid hassani, Alvestrand, Ianneub, Olivier Debre, Moxfyre, Slavik0329, Freakofnurture, Rich Farmbrough, Bender235, Dewet, RJHall, Tjic, Bobo192, Jjmerelo~enwiki, Aquillion, Kjkolb, Krellis, Hooperbloob, ClementSeveillac, Joolz, BodyTag, InShaneee, Juhtolv, Kusma, BDD, Bsdlogical, Yurivict, Feezo, Simetrical, Woohookitty, Mindmatrix, Carlos Porto, Shello, Mihai Damian, Pol098, CiTrusD, JediKnyghte, Josh Parris, Rjwilmsi, PHenry, Yamamoto Ichiro, FlaBot, Latka, Gurch, Intgr, Zebediah49, Benlisquare, Dadu~enwiki, Yurik-Bot, Wavelength, Samuel Wiki, StuffOfInterest, The Literate Engineer, NawlinWiki, Mosquitopsu, Scs, Deku-shrub, Flipjargendy, Romal, Abune, Rurik, Fsiler, Katieh5584, One, SmackBot, Narson, McGeddon, Brick Thrower, KelleyCook, Eiler7, Mcld, Gilliam, Ohnoitsjamie, Chris the speller, Kurykh, TimBentley, Jcc1, Sinicixp, DHN-bot~enwiki, Emurphy42, Jmax-, Can't sleep, clown will eat me, Trinite, Blah2, Mitsuhirato, Frap, JonHarder, Hitoride~enwiki, Luno.org, Rockpocket, Kuru, Euchiasmus, Ivucica, Ehheh, Ttul, Dl2000, Hu12, DabMachine, HisSpaceResearch, Iridescent, Winkydink, KimChee, Powerslide, DavidTangye, Kylu, Dgw, Jesse Viviano, Hserus, RagingR2, Abdullahazzam, Grahamrichter, Mzima, Mato, Gogo Dodo, DumbBOT, Optimist on the run, Zokum, Kozuch, Tobias382, Ferris37, Mbell, Ckhung, Aiko, Bobblehead, OrenBochman, Binarybits, Sidasta, Luna Santin, Tohnayy, Luxomni, Lfstevens, Mscullin, AndreasWittenstein, SemperSecurus, Husond, Sheitan, Struthious Bandersnatch, Andreas Toth, Magioladitis, VoABot II, Nyttend, Upholder, Boffob, Daniel.birket, Ryan1918, Forensicsguy, MartinBot, SasaMaker, LittleOldMe old, Boston, J.delanoy, EscapingLife, Skiidoo, Eliz81, Milo03, Mtxf, Buhadram, Fomalhaut71, Crakkpot, Jwh335, STBotD, Sbanker, VolkovBot, LokiClock, Franck Dernoncourt, Philip Trueman, TXiKiBoT, Stagefrog2, Brian Helsinki, Lambyte, Calculuslover800, Ephix, InFAN1ty, C45207, Senpai71, Michael Frind, Logan, Derekcslater, Sephiroth storm, Yintan, Android Mouse, Exert, Jonahtrainer, KoshVorlon, Lightmouse, IdreamofJeanie, Dracker, Denisarona, Escape Orbit, The sunder king, Mr. Granger, Jaimee212, Church, ClueBot, GorillaWarfare, Abhinav, Vacio, Ravivr, Lawrence Cohen, Konsumkind, Pwitham, Paul Abrahams, Mild Bill Hiccup, DnetSvg, Dante brevity, Rprpr, Julesbarbie, Excirial, Gulmammad, Dralokyn, Rhododendrites, SchreiberBike, DanielPharos, D.Cedric, BlueDevil, Herunar, XLinkBot, Dark Mage, Stickee, Little Mountain 5, WikHead, Jadtnr1, A little mollusk, Addbot, Ramu50, A.qarta, Burkestar, Enkrona, Zellfaze, Tothwolf, Linktopast30, Scientus, MrOllie, Danpoulton, Hintss, Jarble, Luckas-bot, Yobot, Ptbotgourou, AnomieBOT, Jim1138, Yachtsman1, Materialscientist, Hcps-spottsgr, LykMurph, ArthurBot, Quebec99, Xqbot, THWoodman, DataWraith, BebyB, S0aasdf2sf, GrouchoBot, Kyng, Chaheel Riens, FrescoBot, W Nowicki, Chilrreh, HamburgerRadio, 10metreh, Skyerise, Bugsguy, Pastafarian32, GlowBee, Fishsicles, Lbwilliams, Trappist the monk, Dundonite, Lotje, Dragan2~enwiki, Tbhotch, Jfmantis, Onel5969, Liamzebedee, Ripchip Bot, EmausBot, Jackson McArthur, Cmartincaj, Heracles31, ScottyBerg, Dewritech, JohnValeron, RenamedUser01302013, K6ka, Marshviperx, Martinibra, Daonguyen95, A930913, H3llBot, Ivhtbr, Erianna, Staszek Lem, TyA, The guy on da moon, Cyberdog958, Schnoatbrax, Rigley, Donner60, TravisMunson1993, Whoop whoop pull up, Mjbmrbot, Gary Dee, ClueBot NG, Magicman3894, MelbourneStar, Satellizer, Abecedarius, Guive37, Twillisjr, Mgnicholas, Mesoderm, O.Koslowski, Helpful Pixie Bot, Harley16ss, TRANA1-NJITWILL, Lifemaestro, Hewhoamareismyself, Fredo699, Vagobot, DaveB549, Paulbeeb, ElphiBot, MusikAnimal, Socal212, Affinanti3, Szary89, AdventurousSquirrel, Zune0112, Jbarre10, Gyvachius, Tetraflexagon, Haleycat, Cyberbot II, Deimos747, Faisal ALbarrak, Oknitram, Chengshuotian, Padenton, Superkc, Waqob, FoCuSandLeArN, Oneplusnine, Me, Myself, and I are Here, Agent766, Axesrotoor, Jakedtc, Compdewd, FockeWulf FW 190, FrB.TG, Herpingdo, JaconaFrere, Impsswoon, TheEpTic, Jamesmarkchan, AnonArme, Fl4meb0tnet, Professornova, Anotherdaylate, Crystallizedcarbon, Spagheti, Ceannlann gorm, MusikBot, BrainSquared, Yasuo Miyakawa, Kurousagi, UttamSINHA, JohnStew826, Hacktivist117, Sharanyanaveen, Dogeipedia, GreenC bot, Jeaser91, Shraypuri, Ps765330, Jicetus, Truelovefree and Anonymous: 487

- **0x80** *Source:* https://en.wikipedia.org/wiki/0x80?oldid=741146249 *Contributors:* SimonP, Zanimum, Texture, Mattflaschen, Jh51681, Klemen Kocjancic, Qutezuce, Bawolff, CloudNine, H2g2bob, GregorB, ElKevbo, RussBot, Taed, Encephalon, SmackBot, Aim Here, Ratarsed, Rtc, Cesium 133, Paul Foxworthy, Nick Number, RobotG, JaGa, Jlechem, LokiClock, Kumioko (renamed), Arjayay, 1ForTheMoney, Yobot, AnomieBOT, FrescoBot, Super Goku V, Faizanalivarya, Colapeninsula, BattyBot, ChrisGualtieri, KasparBot and Anonymous: 10

- **Akbot** *Source:* https://en.wikipedia.org/wiki/Akbot?oldid=738692982 *Contributors:* Rjwilmsi, XLerate, Wavelength, Shadowblade, VigilancePrime, Hydrogen Iodide, Snori, Magioladitis, Transcendence, Juliancolton, Someguy1221, Ephix, Escape Orbit, Wikilost, Radiofreejohn, Excirial, DanielPharos, LiteralKa, HaleyZZ, Wingman4l7, FockeWulf FW 190, Anarchyte, GreenC bot and Anonymous: 3

- **Alureon** *Source:* https://en.wikipedia.org/wiki/Alureon?oldid=742099820 *Contributors:* Mecanismo, L.Willms, Charonn0, Mduvekot, Sir Joseph, Nneonneo, ElKevbo, DVdm, Tetsuo, Josh3580, Cojoco, SmackBot, General Ization, Mike1901, N2e, Dawnseeker2000, Rebelcommander, Keith D, R'n'B, OttoMäkelä, Oshwah, Wiae, Haseo9999, Laoris, Flyer22 Reborn, Socrates2008, DanielPharos, XLinkBot, Dthomsen8, Addbot, Peridon, Luckas-bot, AnomieBOT, Jim1138, SaturnineMind, Safinaskar, HamburgerRadio, Jcc, Hitfactory, Marcelometal, DASHBot, Will Hawes, EmausBot, Klbrain, Bamyers99, ClueBot NG, Resa1983, Theopolisme, BG19bot, EagerToddler39, Telfordbuck, Class455, Kevinmcguire1, FockeWulf FW 190, Faizan.m, Thibaut120094, Ffaaiizzaann123, Gaelan, Jaylazzara, Satishsahani123, Dachimp78, RyanClaude1972, Film Director In Mumbai, AstridMitch, Wikipenguin 8, Evanstone1, Cvnnyv, Mohamed Abdirizak Dhagow, Wilenson, Inploded, Alyssawaldon, Nekohappi, LovableFool, Mtntime, A.VENKATESH PALAYAKAYAL, Chinnu chandra, Mr.nawa, Isiah.Shive14812, Medialinkp, IZephr, PixelCog, MrE97, Masato Takahashi MD, Lexieee.02l, A south african kid, Erryn Xu, Ksomean35, Happydadnyc, Laurel Palmer, Jew fc, Btalred1, Ak13rox, Jayd5930, Raymond03121, Derp102, Jaiuwulk, Fjordface577, RobertGRAND, Ericlin10, Grammarperson, IsRomero, Suckaassbobdick, Purpletickets, Thetenantdoctor, WolfieCrazy, GreenC bot, EdwardUK and Anonymous: 38

- **Asprox botnet** *Source:* https://en.wikipedia.org/wiki/Asprox_botnet?oldid=745215448 *Contributors:* Pnm, Tabletop, Xaosflux, ArglebargleIV, Hebrides, Excirial, Mortense, Ettrig, Yobot, DASHBot, Peaceray, Brycehughes, Dobie80, Codename Lisa, Pacguy64, GreenC bot and Anonymous: 5

- **Bagle (computer worm)** *Source:* https://en.wikipedia.org/wiki/Bagle_(computer_worm)?oldid=739976807 *Contributors:* Bryan Derksen, Finlay McWalter, David Gerard, Klemen Kocjancic, Trafton, Discospinster, Xezbeth, Martey, A-Day, HasharBot~enwiki, Waldir, Marudubshinki, FlaBot, Eubot, Zotel, Lexi Marie, Barefootguru, SmackBot, KelleyCook, Xaosflux, Wtwilson3, BillFlis, Cydebot, Gogo Dodo, AntiVandalBot, Gavia immer, Arnesh, Tiddly Tom, Soulweaver, Excirial, Seichler, Addbot, Jsmx21, SpBot, Yobot, Piano non troppo, ShadowOdyssey, Hydrozorz, HamburgerRadio, SwineFlew?, Full-date unlinking bot, Bamyers99, ClueBot NG, FockeWulf FW 190, Rampage470, Poprock1539, ToonLucas22, Bikey220 and Anonymous: 29

- **BASHLITE** *Source:* https://en.wikipedia.org/wiki/BASHLITE?oldid=745243299 *Contributors:* FockeWulf FW 190

- **Bot herder** *Source:* https://en.wikipedia.org/wiki/Bot_herder?oldid=671646744 *Contributors:* Darrell Greenwood, Greenrd, McDutchie, Histrion, Rich Farmbrough, Nuggetboy, DoubleBlue, Hm2k, Liastnir, SmackBot, Frap, Robofish, Rdunn, Epbr123, Widefox, Theadesilva, Joewski, Squids and Chips, Loopafiasco, Hutcher, Yobot, Fraggle81, Erik9bot, Pokeatthedevil, Encognito, Pdecalculus and Anonymous: 12

- **Bredolab botnet** *Source:* https://en.wikipedia.org/wiki/Bredolab_botnet?oldid=714447751 *Contributors:* Mr.Unknown, Intgr, Dadu~enwiki, Black Falcon, Flipjargendy, Xaosflux, Chris the speller, Jane023, Grahamec, Hebrides, Smartse, R'n'B, Excirial, Peridon, Materialscientist, Prari, Lotje, Amphicoelias, RjwilmsiBot, Razzattack, Michielderoo, Toaster2010, Freelancer Jerachi, Mgnicholas, BG19bot, Schrödinger's Neurotoxin, PStibbons, 967Bytes, Ahmed.fshosha, Daan degr, BrainSquared and Anonymous: 9

- **Carna botnet** *Source:* https://en.wikipedia.org/wiki/Carna_botnet?oldid=692153998 *Contributors:* Bender235, Wavelength, Qwyrxian, Desc~enwiki, Sitush, Yobot, Diannaa, John of Reading, Tuankiet65, W163, Atlasowa, Jeb the hick, FoCuSandLeArN, Loup Solitaire 81, Lowkeyvision, Fixuture, Themikebest and Anonymous: 4

- **Coreflood** *Source:* https://en.wikipedia.org/wiki/Coreflood?oldid=574511054 *Contributors:* Gracefool, Reisio, Rjwilmsi, Malcolma, MonsieurKovacs, Dimo414, Sun Creator, Addbot, Yobot and Fqi

- **Cutwail botnet** *Source:* https://en.wikipedia.org/wiki/Cutwail_botnet?oldid=722623188 *Contributors:* Fubar Obfusco, Klemen Kocjancic, Rich Farmbrough, Bender235, BD2412, SmackBot, M.S.K., Bonadea, Excirial, DanielPharos, Yobot, Chevymontecarlo, Dcirovic, Wingman4l7, Neøn, MeanMotherJr, Gianlucasb, Chc1987 and Anonymous: 2

- **Domain generation algorithm** *Source:* https://en.wikipedia.org/wiki/Domain_generation_algorithm?oldid=743520067 *Contributors:* Falcon Kirtaran, Utcursch, Mormegil, Frap, Disavian, Ivan Pozdeev, OhanaUnited, Althena, Dekart, Yobot, SwisterTwister, AnomieBOT, Fredatl, ChrisGualtieri, Khazar2, GSMcNamara, FockeWulf FW 190, Dough34, Impsswoon and Anonymous: 8

- **Donbot botnet** *Source:* https://en.wikipedia.org/wiki/Donbot_botnet?oldid=739204337 *Contributors:* JHunterJ, Excirial, Yobot, Peaceray, Werieth, InTheRevolution2, GreenC bot and Anonymous: 1

- **Festi** *Source:* https://en.wikipedia.org/wiki/Festi?oldid=683815810 *Contributors:* Amatulic, Carriearchdale, FrescoBot, Lawsonstu, BattyBot, ChrisGualtieri, SpeedyAstro, WIYoxz107U, Rebeccakcoco and Anonymous: 3

- **Festi botnet** *Source:* https://en.wikipedia.org/wiki/Festi_botnet?oldid=709543591 *Contributors:* Intgr, Excirial, BG19bot, BattyBot and Herpingdo

- **Gameover ZeuS** *Source:* https://en.wikipedia.org/wiki/Gameover_ZeuS?oldid=743783390 *Contributors:* The Anome, David Gerard, Smyth, Arthur Rubin, Abune, Xaosflux, KurtR, Encycloshave, FrederickE, Keepinternetfree, MrScorch6200, FockeWulf FW 190, JohnStew826, Neighbordog and Anonymous: 6

- **Grum botnet** *Source:* https://en.wikipedia.org/wiki/Grum_botnet?oldid=738270080 *Contributors:* Pnm, Wjfox2005, Frap, Ozzieboy, Excirial, Addbot, Joaquin008, TjBot, Lellisinca, Peaceray, Assembled, Wingman4l7, ClueBot NG, Дневной дозор, Ebais, FockeWulf FW 190, Zachary-Keeton and Anonymous: 11

- **Gumblar** *Source:* https://en.wikipedia.org/wiki/Gumblar?oldid=743655796 *Contributors:* Edward, Klemen Kocjancic, Intgr, Abune, SmackBot, Kvng, Atamata, Fabrictramp, VolkovBot, Kroond, Malcolmxl5, Aneeshjoseph, JL-Bot, Dpmuk, Ktr101, Excirial, DanielPharos, W4otn, Addbot, Yobot, KamikazeBot, AnomieBOT, Gpia7r, Netbabu, Shirik, HamburgerRadio, Joe12387, Briansilberberg, Dinamik-bot, John of Reading, Timtempleton, Active Banana, Tommy2010, K6ka, Bamyers99, Wagner, Gumblar Destroyer, WikiPeed-on-ya, FeralOink, TechnoTalk and Anonymous: 21

- **Kelihos botnet** *Source:* https://en.wikipedia.org/wiki/Kelihos_botnet?oldid=704306301 *Contributors:* Vsmith, Bender235, Art LaPella, Crisco 1492, A bit iffy, Ohconfucius, Obiwankenobi, Excirial, Yobot, AnomieBOT, 22Rimfire, Citation bot, Monkbot, Hannasnow, 331468A and Anonymous: 5

- **Kraken botnet** *Source:* https://en.wikipedia.org/wiki/Kraken_botnet?oldid=647019789 *Contributors:* The Anome, Tempshill, Nurg, Klemen Kocjancic, Discospinster, Krellis, GregorB, Riki, SmackBot, Noir~enwiki, Phoenixrod, Weedbag, Jesse Viviano, Smiteri, John254, Anaxial, Davidwr, Ephix, TJRC, Lawrence Cohen, Excirial, NuclearWarfare, LeheckaG, Tsil.swarm, Estudi0loco, Sonofafish, Capricorn42, DataWraith, Ched, Crusoe8181, Fredatl, Neøn and Anonymous: 20

- **Lethic botnet** *Source:* https://en.wikipedia.org/wiki/Lethic_botnet?oldid=705312844 *Contributors:* Pnm, Zootm, Mentifisto, Hvandenberg, Excirial, Peaceray, TomChunata, Lunamia, BG19bot, FockeWulf FW 190 and Anonymous: 3

- **Mariposa botnet** *Source:* https://en.wikipedia.org/wiki/Mariposa_botnet?oldid=739204057 *Contributors:* Neutrality, Vsmith, Bender235, Art LaPella, Giraffedata, Woohookitty, Eleassar, Arthur Rubin, Tom Morris, Xaosflux, Yamaguchi先生, Rlevse, Frap, Khazar, Smartse, Santhosh.thottingal, Excirial, Addbot, Anna Frodesiak, Trappist the monk, Lotje, RjwilmsiBot, H3llBot, Warnis, Widr, BG19bot, Blackberry Sorbet, Tana9408, Cyberbot II, GreenC bot and Anonymous: 13

- **Mega-D botnet** *Source:* https://en.wikipedia.org/wiki/Mega-D_botnet?oldid=646794710 *Contributors:* Nurg, Klemen Kocjancic, Irrbloss, Benlisquare, ImGz, KimChee, BenTels, Excirial, DanielPharos, Dawynn, Download, Dmdicki, Fe4200, Peaceray, Wingman4l7, Neøn, Shedwigs, BattyBot and Anonymous: 9

- **Metulji botnet** *Source:* https://en.wikipedia.org/wiki/Metulji_botnet?oldid=712382914 *Contributors:* Hydrargyrum, Bejnar, XLinkBot, Omniomi, Wagner, Gurt Posh, Miksasike, FockeWulf FW 190 and Anonymous: 2

- **Mevade Botnet** *Source:* https://en.wikipedia.org/wiki/Mevade_Botnet?oldid=731428907 *Contributors:* I dream of horses, FockeWulf FW 190, Karelexor, Gab4gab, Wyrvan and Anonymous: 1

- **Mirai (malware)** *Source:* https://en.wikipedia.org/wiki/Mirai_(malware)?oldid=745449720 *Contributors:* Yobot and FockeWulf FW 190

- **Necurs botnet** *Source:* https://en.wikipedia.org/wiki/Necurs_botnet?oldid=731013838 *Contributors:* Magioladitis, Kcdills, Yobot, BG19bot, FockeWulf FW 190, My Chemistry romantic and TheTruthCreator

- **Nitol botnet** *Source:* https://en.wikipedia.org/wiki/Nitol_botnet?oldid=726555802 *Contributors:* Klemen Kocjancic, Dawnseeker2000, Excirial, Yobot, BattyBot, FockeWulf FW 190 and Anonymous: 3

- **Operation: Bot Roast** *Source:* https://en.wikipedia.org/wiki/Operation%3A_Bot_Roast?oldid=731984500 *Contributors:* Pnm, B.d.mills, Neutrality, Klemen Kocjancic, Bender235, Dachannien, Ricky81682, Yuckfoo, Pauli133, Rjwilmsi, Arthur Rubin, NeilN, SmackBot, C.Fred, KD5TVI, Snori, Reaper X, Onorem, Risker, Eastlaw, Esemono, Gioto, Public Menace, RagnaParadise, SpigotMap, AllGloryToTheHypnotoad, Ephix, Silent52, Blueking12, FlamingSilmaril, ClueBot, Professional Internet User, Lawrence Cohen, Ottre, DanielPharos, AndreNatas, JBsupreme, Bunnyhop11, LifeIsPain, Erik9, HamburgerRadio, Dashren2001, Helpful Pixie Bot, Seafax, BlazeT3ck, DDosFreedomofspeed and Anonymous: 18

- **Rustock botnet** *Source:* https://en.wikipedia.org/wiki/Rustock_botnet?oldid=712359366 *Contributors:* Julesd, Doradus, Pigsonthewing, Wk muriithi, Art LaPella, Smalljim, Pol098, Amitparikh, Ucucha, Hydrargyrum, Gaius Cornelius, Groink, JeffyP, BW95, Leuce, Nyttend, R'n'B, Excirial, Addbot, JackieBot, LilHelpa, Lotje, Jesse V., RjwilmsiBot, EmausBot, Peaceray, TuHan-Bot, ZéroBot, Michael Vastola, Crh23, FockeWulf FW 190, I drink Maria Sharapova's urine, Rover MG, Audiencela and Anonymous: 11

- **Sality** *Source:* https://en.wikipedia.org/wiki/Sality?oldid=739342472 *Contributors:* Klemen Kocjancic, Dennis Brown, Savvo, Gobonobo, Connor Behan, SchreiberBike, FrescoBot, Serols, Jesse V., Sivicia, Werieth, BG19bot, Abc harold, Haleycat, Sumthingood, Faizan, GreenC bot and Anonymous: 8

- **Slenfbot** *Source:* https://en.wikipedia.org/wiki/Slenfbot?oldid=678517099 *Contributors:* Klemen Kocjancic, Yobot, Dewritech, Sumthingood and Anonymous: 1

- **Srizbi botnet** *Source:* https://en.wikipedia.org/wiki/Srizbi_botnet?oldid=738812969 *Contributors:* David Gerard, Art LaPella, Kjkolb, Pauli133, Royan, Riki, Daverocks, Grafen, Bkil, Super Rad!, Incnis Mrsi, McGeddon, Chris the speller, Mungk, JzG, Soap, A. Parrot, Iridescent, Phoenixrod, PamD, Hassocks5489, Struthious Bandersnatch, Nono64, Milo03, Goltz20707, Lightmouse, Ndemou, Excirial, Socrates2008, DanielPharos, Addbot, Felixggenest, Scooty, Ptbotgourou, Jim1138, Aaagmnr, Flewis, J04n, Brutaldeluxe, RjwilmsiBot, Peaceray, H3llBot, Technical 13, Cyberbot II, FockeWulf FW 190, Fabienpe, JohnStew826, GreenC bot and Anonymous: 26

- **Stacheldraht** *Source:* https://en.wikipedia.org/wiki/Stacheldraht?oldid=732176008 *Contributors:* RedWolf, Mushroom, Trafton, CanisRufus, Shaddack, Terra Green, Mooingpolarbear, Trainra, Romal, Sean Whitton, Frap, ShelfSkewed, NapoliRoma, .anacondabot, DanielPharos, Addbot, Killiondude, Capricorn42, HamburgerRadio, Donner60, KScarfone, FockeWulf FW 190, OmniBot and Anonymous: 10

- **Storm botnet** *Source:* https://en.wikipedia.org/wiki/Storm_botnet?oldid=739773441 *Contributors:* General Wesc, The Anome, Michael Hardy, Stefan-S, Nertzy, Tempshill, Nurg, Postdlf, HaeB, Wwoods, Michael Devore, AlistairMcMillan, MisfitToys, Kaldari, OwenBlacker, Rich Farmbrough, D-Notice, Bender235, PhilHibbs, Bobo192, Krellis, Axl, VladimirKorablin, Ronark, Reinoutr, Woohookitty, Mindmatrix, Pol098, ^demon, Rjwilmsi, Jamie Kitson, PHenry, Volty, Jehochman, Bmenrigh, AySz88, RobertG, Riki, Alfadog, Wavelength, Brandmeister (old), RussBot, Ventolin, Eleassar, Bovineone, Superiority, 21655, JQF, BorgQueen, Harthacnut, Twilight Realm, SmackBot, VigilancePrime, Frap, Juancnuno, Deathsythe, Romanski, Rgawenda, Harryboyles, Kuru, Writtenonsand, Adj08, Tktktk, 16@r, Smith609, Optakeover, AdultSwim, Travia21, Lee Carre, Ivan Pozdeev, FunPika, Wafulz, Eric, W guice, Jesse Viviano, Surfbum, Arrenlex, Phatom87, Asenine, Kozuch, Scarpy, Hairmare, N5iln, X201, SusanLesch, Stybn, Dekkanar, JamzYaneza, Jj137, Jadelmann, Uneautrepoire, Danger, Qwerty Binary, Ingolfson, MER-C, Schlegel, Andonic, Hewinsj, Dragonnas, Unused0029, VoABot II, AuburnPilot, Zoombody, Adrian J. Hunter, GermanX, Kestasjk, Navyteacher86, Ultraviolet scissor flame, Ryan.hunt, R'n'B, RockMFR, J.delanoy, DrKay, Gaming4JC, Maurice Carbonaro, Public Menace, FrummerThanThou, Pyrospirit, Sarregouset, X!, The Duke of Waltham, Davidwr, GimmeBot, Liko81, Doomaholic, From-cary, Rjm at sleepers, McM.bot, Ephix, Silent52, Meters, Sweeces, Jbmurray, Calabraxthis, Jerryobject, Arbor to SJ, Eóin, Lightmouse, Meatydude, Svick, LarRan, FlamingSilmaril, ClueBot, DarkAvZ, Lawrence Cohen, Arbeit Sockenpuppe, Cirt, Noca2plus, Drydom, Yemal, Aron4000, Promethean, Razorflame, Rhetzky, Herunar, XLinkBot, LeheckaG, Zodon, Addbot, Matthrkac, Majortried 483,dkvjtmtk34, Samsim123, Sam8888, A.qarta, LinkFA-Bot, PopularOutcast, Lightbot, Kuzetsa, Dalek9, AnomieBOT, Sz-iwbot, Chcantre, 口口口口, Vanatom, FrescoBot, LatchLinksMen, HamburgerRadio, Calmer Waters, DASHBot, Orphan Wiki, Tmarie08, GoingBatty, H3llBot, Music Sorter, 28bot, Zxcvbn1701, J.Dong820, Technical 13, Mark Arsten, Kabritu, Cyberbot II, Dexbot, Me, Myself, and I are Here, FockeWulf FW 190, Iwilsonp, Ethan010, JohnStew826, GreenC bot and Anonymous: 111

- **Torpig** *Source:* https://en.wikipedia.org/wiki/Torpig?oldid=736522713 *Contributors:* Cb6, Hoary, Hydrargyrum, Welsh, Dave Dugal, M3taphysical, SmackBot, Yamaguchi口口, Gilliam, Gogo Dodo, DumbBOT, Utopiah, Widefox, Finchut.2011, Excirial, Socrates2008, DanielPharos, SF007, XLinkBot, Addbot, Yobot, Commander Shepard, Capricorn42, HamburgerRadio, Cedricpernet, TobeBot, K6ka, ZéroBot, Wagner, ClueBot NG, AdventurousSquirrel, FockeWulf FW 190, Aashrayarora, DatGuy, JudgeRM, Lovesharma0061 and Anonymous: 28

- **Tribe Flood Network** *Source:* https://en.wikipedia.org/wiki/Tribe_Flood_Network?oldid=715145112 *Contributors:* Abune, SmackBot, Frap, Alekjds, OlEnglish, FockeWulf FW 190 and Anonymous: 3

- **Trinoo** *Source:* https://en.wikipedia.org/wiki/Trinoo?oldid=738394488 *Contributors:* Zundark, Rich Farmbrough, Mike Schwartz, Csabo, Ahazred8, Reisio, Abune, SmackBot, Frap, Dougher, Goldenglove, Alekjds, R'n'B, GuzzoMEcrazy, Ottre, DanielPharos, AnomieBOT, Spidern, ClueBot NG, BG19bot, KScarfone, Shaun, Cyberbot II, Sam Sailor, FockeWulf FW 190, Monkbot, GreenC bot and Anonymous: 14

- **United States v. Ancheta** *Source:* https://en.wikipedia.org/wiki/United_States_v._Ancheta?oldid=716577047 *Contributors:* Cmdrjameson, Giraffedata, BD2412, Rjwilmsi, Ground Zero, George Ho, Mild Bill Hiccup, Ottawahitech, Yobot, Srich32977, Dewritech, Gorthian and Pdhadialla

- **Virut** *Source:* https://en.wikipedia.org/wiki/Virut?oldid=721741988 *Contributors:* Markhurd, Piotrus, Mindmatrix, Rjwilmsi, Excirial, ClueBot NG, Codename Lisa, NYBrook098, FockeWulf FW 190, Pacguy and Anonymous: 2

- **Vulcanbot** *Source:* https://en.wikipedia.org/wiki/Vulcanbot?oldid=625335426 *Contributors:* Green Giant, Niceguyedc, DanielPharos, Ironholds, Tassedethe, Tijfo098 and Enfcer

- **Waledac botnet** *Source:* https://en.wikipedia.org/wiki/Waledac_botnet?oldid=726574848 *Contributors:* Klemen Kocjancic, Slampaladino, BenTels, Excirial, Addbot, AnomieBOT, BenzolBot, RjwilmsiBot, Peaceray, Aman majestic, BG19bot, Cyberbot II, FockeWulf FW 190 and Anonymous: 7

- **Xor DDoS** *Source:* https://en.wikipedia.org/wiki/Xor_DDoS?oldid=732179449 *Contributors:* Hebrides, Garagepunk66, FockeWulf FW 190, OmniBot and Anonymous: 1

- **ZeroAccess botnet** *Source:* https://en.wikipedia.org/wiki/ZeroAccess_botnet?oldid=739401256 *Contributors:* Esrogs, Pol098, A bit iffy, Chris the speller, FredWallace18@yahoo.com, Jesse Viviano, Gogo Dodo, SnootyClaus, Dawnseeker2000, Denisarona, Excirial, Rhododendrites, XLinkBot, Canberranone, FrescoBot, Gary Dee, BG19bot, Paganinip, BattyBot, ChrisGualtieri, EuroCarGT, Andyhowlett, FockeWulf FW 190, Frenzie23, Cdlobban, Antrocent, 1Wiki8Q5G7FviTHBac3dx8HhdNYwDVstR, Invisible Guy, GreenC bot and Anonymous: 27

- **Zeus (malware)** *Source:* https://en.wikipedia.org/wiki/Zeus_(malware)?oldid=742733478 *Contributors:* The Anome, William Avery, Delirium, Discospinster, Vsmith, Bender235, Smalljim, TheSolomon, Wtmitchell, Woohookitty, Pol098, RomeW, BD2412, DVdm, Rwalker, Arthur Rubin, NeilN, SmackBot, C.Fred, Yamaguchi⬜⬜, Mcld, Vvarkey, Skiminki, Ian Dalziel, Dl2000, Jesse Viviano, Rajendra bn, Gogo Dodo, DumbBOT, Utopiah, Gioto, Widefox, Smartse, Magioladitis, Nyttend, Philg88, J.delanoy, Ritual, Derekrogerson, Mufka, Bonadea, SoCalSuperEagle, Philip Trueman, Wiae, Falcon8765, Michael Frind, Mehmet Karatay, Copana2002, Mikemoral, Happysailor, Flyer22 Reborn, Capitalismojo, ImageRemovalBot, Sfan00 IMG, Halcyonforever, Boing! said Zebedee, Ansh666, Excirial, Socrates2008, Muhandes, Pot, SoxBot, DanielPharos, Crnorizec, WikHead, Bookbrad, Addbot, Mortense, Jojhutton, Haggistech, Tyw7, 84user, Luckas-bot, Yobot, AnomieBOT, DemocraticLuntz, JackieBot, Nasnema, Kylelovesyou, Lena from Kiev, Alarics, HamburgerRadio, BasisBit, I dream of horses, Andrewigoss, Lotje, Mean as custard, RjwilmsiBot, Darth Stabro, EmausBot, Dewritech, GoingBatty, Peaceray, K6ka, Bollyjeff, Briangirardi, H3llBot, Simpatico qa, GeorgeBarnick, Brandmeister, L Kensington, Kenny Strawn, Rocketrod1960, ClueBot NG, Sabre ball, Jeraphine Gryphon, Phnom-Pencil, Neøn, AdventurousSquirrel, TheRedVendetta, Wolverinebb4l, Glacialfox, Cyberbot II, ChrisGualtieri, Rezonansowy, AaronMP84, Vicious1337, Frosty, Graphium, Kevin12xd, Cool12248, MountRainier, A Certain Lack of Grandeur, Jackmcbarn, FockeWulf FW 190, Bigdatavomit, Vieque, Seankclark, ChamithN, PawnTeeth, Liance, FourViolas, Kartikay sp, Sagar16111991, Mrcult47, Gary1991420, Andie Criz, Kursk2012, Jamesanderson90, Mikebilz, Kevin dalton1, Jeraphine, My Chemistry romantic, Yasuo Miyakawa, Roy Downey, Wiki Guy 5045, Sahils4400, Amarsethi2015, Ammywatson007, Sonu14581, PAUL14581, Sonu145819, Firebrace, Barah123, Raveesh005, InternetArchiveBot, GreenC bot, Plaindinks and Anonymous: 130

46.7.2 Images

- **File:0x80_cracker_with_laptop.jpg** *Source:* https://upload.wikimedia.org/wikipedia/en/f/fe/0x80_cracker_with_laptop.jpg *License:* Fair use *Contributors:* URL: http://www.washingtonpost.com/wp-dyn/content/article/2006/02/14/AR2006021401342_5.html This image is from a *Washington Post* article called "Invasion of the Computer Snatchers" about a cracker named 0x80 who creates botnets which are used to install spyware for a commission. *Original artist: Washington Post* (Unidentified photographer)

- **File:Ambox_current_red.svg** *Source:* https://upload.wikimedia.org/wikipedia/commons/9/98/Ambox_current_red.svg *License:* CC0 *Contributors:* self-made, inspired by Gnome globe current event.svg, using Information icon3.svg and Earth clip art.svg *Original artist:* Vipersnake151, penubag, Tkgd2007 (clock)

- **File:Ambox_important.svg** *Source:* https://upload.wikimedia.org/wikipedia/commons/b/b4/Ambox_important.svg *License:* Public domain *Contributors:* Own work, based off of Image:Ambox scales.svg *Original artist:* Dsmurat (talk · contribs)

- **File:Ambox_wikify.svg** *Source:* https://upload.wikimedia.org/wikipedia/commons/e/e1/Ambox_wikify.svg *License:* Public domain *Contributors:* Own work *Original artist:* penubag

- **File:Carnabotnet_geovideo_lowres.gif** *Source:* https://upload.wikimedia.org/wikipedia/commons/1/1a/Carnabotnet_geovideo_lowres.gif *License:* Public domain *Contributors:* http://internetcensus2012.bitbucket.org/images/geovideo_lowres.gif , [1] *Original artist:* Author of Carna Botnet "Internet Census 2012", PGP public key

- **File:Circle_of_spam.svg** *Source:* https://upload.wikimedia.org/wikipedia/commons/0/08/Circle_of_spam.svg *License:* CC-BY-SA-3.0 *Contributors:* own work, based on png version from English-language Wikipedia (by Fubar Obfusco & Admrboltz) *Original artist:* odder

- **File:Commons-logo.svg** *Source:* https://upload.wikimedia.org/wikipedia/en/4/4a/Commons-logo.svg *License:* CC-BY-SA-3.0 *Contributors:* ? *Original artist:* ?

- **File:Edit-clear.svg** *Source:* https://upload.wikimedia.org/wikipedia/en/f/f2/Edit-clear.svg *License:* Public domain *Contributors:* ? *Original artist:* ?

- **File:Emoji_u1f4bb.svg** *Source:* https://upload.wikimedia.org/wikipedia/commons/d/d7/Emoji_u1f4bb.svg *License:* Apache License 2.0 *Contributors:* https://code.google.com/p/noto/ *Original artist:* Google

- **File:Emojione_1F46E.svg** *Source:* https://upload.wikimedia.org/wikipedia/commons/e/ea/Emojione_1F46E.svg *License:* CC BY-SA 4.0 *Contributors:* https://github.com/Ranks/emojione *Original artist:* https://github.com/Ranks/emojione/graphs/contributors

- **File:FBI_Fraud_Scheme_Zeus_Trojan.jpg** *Source:* https://upload.wikimedia.org/wikipedia/commons/2/2d/FBI_Fraud_Scheme_Zeus_Trojan.jpg *License:* Public domain *Contributors:* FBI *Original artist:* FBI [1]

- **File:Malware_logo.svg** *Source:* https://upload.wikimedia.org/wikipedia/commons/f/ff/Malware_logo.svg *License:* LGPL *Contributors:* Skull and crossbones.svg (valid SVG)
  Original artist: Skull and crossbones.svg: Silsor

- **File:Monitor_padlock.svg** *Source:* https://upload.wikimedia.org/wikipedia/commons/7/73/Monitor_padlock.svg *License:* CC BY-SA 3.0 *Contributors:* Own work (Original text: *self-made*) *Original artist:* Lunarbunny (talk)

- **File:P2P-network.svg** *Source:* https://upload.wikimedia.org/wikipedia/commons/3/3f/P2P-network.svg *License:* Public domain *Contributors:* Own work *Original artist:* User:Mauro Bieg

- **File:P_vip.svg** *Source:* https://upload.wikimedia.org/wikipedia/en/6/69/P_vip.svg *License:* PD *Contributors:* ? *Original artist:* ?

- **File:Question_book-new.svg** *Source:* https://upload.wikimedia.org/wikipedia/en/9/99/Question_book-new.svg *License:* Cc-by-sa-3.0 *Contributors:* ? *Original artist:* ?

46.7.3   Content license